Ripples of Life

Ripples
Of
Life

LaChelle Burroughs

Accountability is the highest form of self-respect and respect of others to me. This is my story. My life. My memories.

I have held myself accountable in these pages. Some names and places have been changed to protect the innocent and maintain their privacy.

Copyright © 2025 by LaChelle Burroughs

All rights reserved. No part of this book may be reproduced or used in any manner without written permission of the copyright owner except for the use of quotations in a book review.

For permission, email the author:

ripplesoflifebook@hotmail.com

ISBN 979-8-218-84711-1 (Paperback)

ISBN 979-8-218-84712-8 (eBook)

All scriptures are from the New King James Version.

Book Cover Design: LaChelle Burroughs

Printed in the United States

Trigger Warnings

Dear Reader,

This book contains the following in no particular order.

    Abortion

    Rape

    Attempted suicide

    Suicidal ideation

    Suicidal ideation involving kids

    Infant death

    Domestic violence

    Self-harm

    Disturbing thoughts

    Sex

    Drugs *although legal in some states*

    Smoking

But God!

As you go with me through my journey, please take care of yourself. If any of the above triggers cause hurt, pain or reflection; I'm sorry. I hope that maybe a song, a word or a prayer brings you closer to the One that is keeping you. And He has Kept you because you are still here reading the words that I typed.

Be Blessed.

LaChelle Burroughs

This book is dedicated to God. My Father. My Savior. My Creator. My Redeemer. My Friend.

There are not enough Thank You's to let you know my gratitude for always Loving me through my worst times, my greatest moments, and all the in-betweens.

May Your Mercy and Grace come across the pages of this book.

May Your Glory be Magnified.

And may I get it right someday.

Table of Contents

Book One

Chapter 1:	Foundations	3
Chapter 2:	This Little Girl	7
Chapter 3:	Misdirected Anger	13
Chapter 4:	Slow Down	17
Chapter 5:	Oh! He Cute	21
Chapter 6:	Faulty Anticipation	25
Chapter 7:	Snow on the Ground	31
Chapter 8:	Time to Choose	37
Chapter 9:	Higher Education	43

Book Two

Chapter 10:	Love at First Sight	51
Chapter 11:	We Have an Issue	57
Chapter 12:	Should've Just Read My Bible	65
Chapter 13:	Lessons Not Learned	73
Chapter 14:	Stay Right Where You Are	79
Chapter 15:	Untitled	92
Chapter 16:	Khalil	96
Chapter 17:	Little Faith	102
Chapter 18:	The Reality of Life	106
Chapter 19:	Please Be Quiet	110

Chapter 20:	Glitches in Sanity	118
Chapter 21:	Time is an Oxymoron	125
Chapter 22:	The Power of a Game	131

Book Three

Chapter 23:	Not in Brooklyn Anymore	137
Chapter 24:	New Address	143
Chapter 25:	Mommy Dearest	145
Chapter 26:	Who Am I?	149
Chapter 27:	Life Goes On	157
Chapter 28:	Regression	159
Chapter 29:	At the Altar	167

Book Four

Chapter 30:	Hidden Behind Destiny	177
Chapter 31:	Classes? What Classes?	185
Chapter 32:	One Day I'll Get It Right	191
Chapter 33:	Silence Can Be a Trigger	199
Chapter 34:	Damn Luther Vandross	203
Chapter 35:	Night on the Town	207
Chapter 36:	A New Theory	212

Introduction

I started this journey twelve years ago while waiting to finalize my divorce.

My life was a mess, and I was trying to clean it up on my own. I had my music going, cold beers in the fridge and a fresh pack of cigarettes. As I would pick up items to put away or throw out, I would get distracted by the memories and emotions. Never able to make a dent to the mess. Things on the counters, chairs, tables and floors. My life was everywhere.

Then I heard a knock at the door. Frantic because I wasn't expecting company, I yelled "just a second" trying to move things out of the way. But distractions would take hold, and I'd forget about the person at the door. Time passed and I never seemed ready to open it. Piles were increasing instead of decreasing. But the person kept knocking.

After a while I gave up. The knocking became annoying, and I realized they were not going to leave me alone. So, I went to the door stepping over mounds of happiness and hurt.

"Hey come in. Forgive the mess. I was trying to straighten up but it's just not working." I said while avoiding blowing smoke in his face. I offered him a beer and he declined.

"I can order a pizza if you'd help me clean up."

"Do you have any fish." He said with a smirk.

"Really? Fish? Thought you'd be tired of that. How long were you out there?"

"Ah, you can never tire of fish, too many ways to make it. And as for your question, I told you in *Revelation 3:20. Behold I stand at the door and knock. If anyone hears my voice and opens the door, I will come in to him and dine with him, and he with Me.* I was just waiting for you to answer."

"You should have shouted. You know the power of distractions."

"And you know I'm more powerful than any distraction."

"Yes and like your friend says in Romans 7:19 and I'm paraphrasing here. When I want to do right I don't but continue doing the sin I beat myself up for doing. Hence, this mess."

"That is why my Father sent Me, and I gave you My Holy Spirit. You can't live this life alone. Now let's start cleaning things up. I want better for you." He said with compassion.

Then together, Jesus and I started creating order. He helped me to see what things I was holding onto that should have been thrown away. Things I should forgive myself for to make room for good things. I cried, talked, cursed and yelled. He listened and guided me while giving me nuggets of wisdom. He even tried to give me parables and each time I just looked at him and said, "not today Jesus. Not today." He didn't listen.

Most importantly, He was patient, understanding and empathetic. Able to relate to every emotion.

My life isn't spotless, nor will it ever be. But because of Him, it's cleaner than before.

He wants to do the same for you. All you must do is open the door.

BOOK ONE

Foundations

It was the middle of ninth grade when my attempt at suicide failed. I was a fourteen-year-old senior in junior high school, looking forward to high school with equal parts excitement and anxiety. That year, I was on the yearbook committee, a cheerleader, and played the flute in band class. I was an honors student, who made A's and A+'s and sometimes a B would show up but not stay long. I was proud of my grades, but there was emptiness inside.

Near the end of eighth grade, my classmate Derrick and I decided to date. Which just meant we hung out, played handball, fooled around, ate lunch and walked to and from school together sometimes holding hands.

In my spare time, I read. Harlequin Romances, and anything by Stephen King, Mary Higgins Clark, Dean Koontz and various other authors. I loved stepping away from my life to get lost in the pages of a book.

At church, I was just as active.

I served on the usher board and sang in the choir. *I only had one solo because my voice shook too much.* When we put on the play *The Wiz*, I was part of the dance team. Dancing was the only time the tremors weren't noticeable. If they were, hopefully it was to the beat of the music. If I participated in the monthly youth service, I would either read the announcements or the scriptures. *If they were short.*

My mom made sure to take my sister and I to every service including the ones all over the city where our Pastor was guest preaching. We also attended Sunday School and Bible Study every week.

It's not bad when the church is of medium size and filled with generational families. My cousins Carlos and Samantha (who are around my sister and I's age), their parents, grandparents and great grandparents also attended the same church. Of course there were other families as well as some of our neighborhood friends. Bible study was the only time it wasn't filled with kids/teens, but on Sundays....it was on and poppin'.

During service, we were loud because we didn't whisper well, and more than a few times; our Pastor would stop service to separate us. Even mid-sermon! But it was ok because after church, while we waited on the adults, we headed to the Bodega for heros, chips and sodas. Creating more noise with laughter and stories from the week and past times together.

In both settings, the only trouble I got in was because of my mouth. I had no respect for authority and didn't care what I said to them. Examples of my mouth getting me into trouble:

    Third grade – Not sure what I said to the teacher, but I do know I was taken in the closet and received several lashings with the ruler across my behind. I think it was only in private schools where the teachers were allowed to physically discipline the students.

    Fourth Grade – For some reason, the kids who attended private school and then public school became the automatic recipient of bullying. Since the teacher did nothing to stop it, I would act out and be disrespectful to him. My mom thought it was best to spank me in front of the class since I was being fresh in front of these same classmates. This only increased the bullying which increased the fighting. *One time I got kicked in the face by this girl going into school.*

Ninth Grade – I yelled, "Fuck You" to my English teacher (who I liked) after being reprimanded for disrupting his class. Again, my mom made me apologize. In front of the whole class!

In church – Most all the adults had no problem telling me to watch my mouth. After all, this was when discipline and correction came from any and everyone who had your best interest in mind. Community Raising. Back when you called the friends of your parents and grandparents Uncle and Auntie out of respect.

If you're thinking that this sounds pretty good, why would I want to kill myself? It was good. However, when you spend your days masking deep hurt from rejection, it's bound to explode.

This Little Girl

I was raised by my mother alongside my sister Regina who is two years older.

We lived in an apartment in the Bushwick section of Brooklyn on the same block as my fraternal grandparents. My grandma, known only to me and Regina as TT, was a beautiful southern debutant that relocated to Brooklyn with her husband whom we called Papa. She wore heels, fur and leather skirts and was always color-coordinated from her earrings to her shoes and pocketbooks. When she traded in the old brown Volkswagen that us kids rode in the trunk part without seatbelts for a Lincoln Town Car, it added to her classiness.

My grandfather was this tall light-skinned man with a head full of curly hair that he allowed Regina and I to play in. He used to bring me fresh flowers every weekend. He bought me a puppy when I was five who died after getting hit by a car. His little demon chihuahua terrorized my childhood with his insistent barking. *Probably why I grew up with a fear of dogs.*

Because of proximity, they spoiled me. It also helped that I was the oldest grandchild on their side. I love my grandparents with every piece of me even though they left this earth too early for my liking. *Thankfully I get to speak with TT quite often in my dreams.*

<u>Examples of a Dad</u>

Regina's father frequently came around and was always nice to me. He never made me feel left out or unacknowledged. On my birthday and for Christmas, he would give me money or a small gift.

He was the one to take me to the hospital when it was time to have Kamar. Probably not the best choice as he was a slow and cautious driver. No matter how much pain the contractions were causing, he was not about to drive over the speed limit.

Other than that, he was always cool to me. I have no negative feelings towards him.

I'm Just a Seed

Lawrence, my father, was the product of TT's first marriage. He was handsome with a smile so wide that you couldn't help but feel special when he smiled at you. He resembled a darker version of Billy Dee Williams. From the afro to the smile. I loved my father, although he was unable to love me. Hence aiding in my unhappiness and the reason I acted out.

As a little girl when Lawrence would tell me he was coming to spend the day with me. I would sit on the radiator in front of the window watching for his arrival. Waiting for him as the kids played in the summertime and in the winter. Looking out for him in the faces of the people that walked up and down the block. If I had a toy or book to keep me occupied, I'd always glance out the window to make sure I didn't miss him. Sometimes I'd stick my head out to get a better view of the block to see if he was coming so I could run out and greet him.

As the hours passed, I would think of things that caused him to be late. The bus broke down. The train stopped running. He couldn't get off work early. When it was warm and my friends wanted me to come outside. I would stay close to the house, so I wouldn't miss him. When I came back inside, I would resume my post. *This went on for too many years I care to remember.* My mom would tell me to "get from in front of that window" or "close my window", and I'd protest. Regina would make nasty comments like, "my dad is here so who you looking for?"

There were times he would call to let me know he wouldn't make it. Most times, he just wouldn't show. It was during these occasions that I would take my disappointment out on my mother and sister. If my sister and I were fighting, she would always win by stating:

> "At least I have a father who loves me"
> "Your dad doesn't even want to see you. Only his mom."
> "Everyone on the block spoke to Lawrence. Did you?"

I started hating her because of slick comments like this. *To this day, she denies she said these types of things.*

As I grew up, my self-esteem did not. My view of myself was that I was ugly. My face was ugly, and my smile was even uglier. When I laughed, I would cover my face with my hands to hide the dimples that were the mirror image of Lawrence. Think of the movie *The Color Purple* when Celie covered her face when she and Shug Avery were in the bedroom standing in front of the mirror.

This view of myself came from a defining moment that took place when I was seven years old. My aunt (no blood relation except she was one of TT's best friends) and I were walking to TTs, and she was talking about the way Lawrence lies. Saying how she thought he was such a snake for the number of fibs he told. In the middle of her bashing him, she looked right at me and said, "It's too bad you look exactly like him. He is ugly inside and out."

With that comment, how could I see myself as anything other than ugly? Especially when I looked just like him. And I didn't think he was ugly. But if the adults did, then where did that leave me? When the adults would talk negatively about him, I listened. I didn't stand up for him because only truth was being spoken. And even when I added in my two cents, the gossip didn't make me feel better. I might have felt good that I wasn't the only one he lied to, but I was the only one that was his child. These conversations always made me feel ugly, unwanted and unloved. *This is why I have NEVER spoken ill about my children's dads around them or to them. I know the damage listening to that stuff does. It sits in your soul and becomes a damaged part of you that is hard to rebuild.*

Even now, I still unconsciously cover my face when I laugh. When I realize I'm covering my face, I remove my hands because I no longer harbor those feelings towards myself. I have come to appreciate my dimples. Now taking pictures is a different story. *Trying to overcome that one.*

To be fair, he did show up sometimes. He even took me to his girlfriend Julia's apartment. But once there, he paid me no mind. His girlfriend, however, became a very good friend to me and I loved her for it. When he left, we'd share stories about his lies. I always won sympathy from her because I was just a child who wanted her father's attention.

One birthday stands out to me. He left a loose-leaf paper folded up in the mailbox that simply said in the center:

Happy Birthday
Love Your Dad

Two quarters were taped on the paper below the message. Enough for two twenty-five cent bags of chips, or a candy bar, or a bag of chips and a quarter water. I took off the coins and threw the note in the trash after showing it to my mom and TT.

One time in fifth grade, I got into a fight with a classmate. When the school called my mother, Lawrence came in her place. Out on the playground, my teacher came up to me and asked if my father was a detective. I laughed and asked him,

"What would make you ask that?"
"He came to the school with a gun on his holster saying he was working a case and stopped by."

I laughed again and told him, "No one knows where he works because the only thing he's good at is lying and making up stories. I'm surprised he even came here."

Mr. Bozzano's response is one that has stayed with me, "That explains your behavior," and walked away. It stayed with me because I didn't understand and mulled over it for days. What he figured out in less than five minutes took me years to grasp.

Lawrence talked with me later that day when I got home. He wanted me to know how to protect myself the next time I got into a fight.

"When you are arguing, and they start to get in your face, change your tone on them. Start speaking softly towards the ground. That is going to confuse them for a minute because you are now calm. If they hit you, don't move. Just stand there. Let them hit you again and still don't hit back. They are not going to know what you are doing. After that second hit and you still haven't moved or said anything, they are going to pause because they thought you were fighting. That pause is when you punch them in the face with all your might."

I must admit, I took his advice the next time I got into a fight. I started speaking softly and calmly looking towards the ground. I took two hits to the face and then swung. We were fighting when the teachers came over and broke us up. After that, I only utilized the first part of his advice. The second part?

I'm not letting anyone get a second hit on me. Anything after the first is self-defense.

Misdirected Anger

When Regina and I physically fought, I would scratch my arms, face, and neck. Digging deep enough for blood to come streaming out. I also pulled out strands of my hair then blamed it all on her. *I stopped this around twelve.* It seemed that was the only way to get her into trouble. Unfortunately, it wasn't a lot of trouble. *And I know my mom didn't think I was doing it to myself because I asked her, and she had no clue.* We'd be yelling and pointing fingers at each other and all Regina would get is a reprimand. Me? I was told, "that's what happens when you fight."

Now as a mom, one of them is lying. I would bet on the one that said they didn't do the scratching. Let my mother even think I was lying, and I got the belt where every lash was its own word. Example: Didn't (lash) - I (lash) - tell (lash) – you (lash) – not (lash).... you get it. *And don't cry. But cry. Because if you don't, they don't stop until you do.*

Why was this dynamic so lopsided? *And still is to this day.* Because Regina was the golden child.

Very respectful and has a beautiful singing voice that didn't shake. She played Dorothy in *The Wiz*, and everyone loved to hear her sing. Even when I couldn't stand her, I would get a sense of pride and adoration when she belted out a tune. *I still do, but please don't tell her. She won't find out unless you tell. Her and our mom told me they are not going to read this because they know everything I'm going to speak about. Or so they think.*

Regina wasn't one to hang outside but stayed indoors with her friends. You would rarely find her outside sitting on the stoop. There was an incident when we shared a room. We were arguing about something, and I took the scissors and cut the cord of her lamp. *And don't groan, I was only around eight or nine.* The problem with my action was that the lamp was plugged in and on. The sparks that flew still have me hesitant to deal with electrical matters.

One time she was chasing me through the house and when I slammed the door in her face, her arm went right through the glass. I couldn't get out of that one since her arm was badly bleeding. So much so that we had to go down the block to an aunt's house (no relation) to get her cleaned up. And to receive my lashing. *Remember, the Community Raising. And yes. My aunt made me pick out my own switch, but I deserved that one. Sort of.*

When these older girls on the block wanted to jump me, she wouldn't come from a friend's house to take up my defense. One of my best friends', her younger brother and a few of his friends showed up on my block with bats to ensure it would be a fair fight. Vaseline was rubbed on my face, neck and arms, and earrings removed, but we didn't fight. The girl snatched off her wig showing off an un-finished hairstyle and the guys started clowning on her. I could not keep a serious face enough to fight with the jokes being made.

Let me insert here that Regina and I didn't always fight. We used to play church in our playroom.

Our stuffed animals were the congregation, she was the choir, and I was the pastor preaching the word to all of them. We would crumble up crackers and have juice for communion. As we got older, she did my hair and helped me pick out outfits. She would sing along with the records, and I'd be her backup dancer. And when she innocently washed my hair with dishwashing liquid, God sent TT over. Her knocking interrupted Regina just as she was about to get the blow-dryer to dry my still soaking wet hair. *She doesn't remember the blow-dryer part but since TT is unable to clear up the memory and it's my book; we are going with how I remember it.*

It was only when we started arguing that she never argued fairly. But then, Lawrence made it easy for her. Like the times we found out he came on the block to visit TT and didn't stop by to see me (remember, we lived on the same block). Those were the things she threw in my face.

She Got it Also

Because of Lawrence, my relationship with my mother was also difficult.

I blamed her whenever he wouldn't show. Thinking things like he couldn't get through on the phone because she was on it. Before we had call waiting, her calls came first. The child in me didn't see the fairness in that. Another reason I blamed her was because they didn't get along. I figured it was why he wouldn't come over to see his daughter.

Because I didn't know how to channel the anger I had for him at him, I directed it to my mom and Regina. I felt like my mother didn't really love me even though she told me I was priceless to her. So priceless that if I were ever to be held for a ransom, she would not pay. "No amount of money would be worth your life." Too bad I spent countless thoughts on how if the ransom was one hundred or two thousand, she wouldn't pay. I'd ask,

"Not even ten dollars?"
"Your life is more than ten dollars so no I would not pay. You are priceless."

It didn't make me feel priceless. It made me feel unwanted. Not even worth ten bucks. It didn't help that Regina convinced me I was adopted. Picked up as a baby and for two years, my mom was trying to give me back. The belief of this lie was accomplished due to my mother not having any photos of me prior to turning two.

So, I talked back. Cursed, *under my breath, I wasn't stupid*, made a fuss when asked to do something, and lied. A lot. Wait. Before I go on, I must tell you about the time when I did call my mom a bitch to her face. My face hit the wall so fast I forgot where I was. I tried to clean it up by asking, "Why you slap me? A bitch is a good thing. A bitch is a female dog and dogs bark, and bark is a tree, and a tree is a living thing. I called you a living thing." She didn't fall for it.

One day while I was doing the dishes, a plate broke. My mother yelled at me for being clumsy and breaking her dish. I was upset that she cared more about the plate than me that when she turned her back, I quickly took a broken piece and sliced my leg. Then I yelled, "You are more concerned about the plate and didn't even notice the blood running down my leg?" She was apologetic as she tended to my self-inflicted wound. *Because of my actions, to this day, if I start yelling at my kids over broken dishes or glasses, my tone changes fast because my mind goes immediately back to this.*

However, being disrespectful wasn't the only way I acted out.

Slow Down

In the seventh grade, I would go around the corner to one of my best friends house, Nicole. She lived across the street from our friend Malik who was a grade higher than us. This made seeing him easy. I would say I was going around the corner to her house, when I really was going to see him. His parents gave him the basement to entertain his friends.

Nicole and I would hang out watching movies on VHS with them. On one of the many days that Lawrence said he couldn't come and see me, but I found out he had visited with TT, I went over to Malik's house. I was his only visitor and since he was my friend, I cried my hurt to him. While I was crying, he lifted my head and kissed me. No tongue, just a soft kiss on the lips. I was stunned and intrigued, no longer crying. When he went to plant another one, it was returned forgetting all about Lawrence. This was not my first kiss. That happened on the playground at Julia's place when I was nine from her neighbor Mickey.

When Malik put his hand up my shirt, I didn't stop him. When his hand found his way in my jeans, I stopped him. I started thinking about how angry Lawrence would be if he found out I was allowing this. As I voiced this to Malik, he responded, "He probably wouldn't even care." That made me mad, so I left. To say he wouldn't care put a voice to what I knew but always hoped wasn't true.

The next time I saw Lawrence; I told him I had a boyfriend, and he yelled at me that I better not be doing anything with him. I was confused at his reaction. Did he really care about me? As he went on yelling that his daughter wasn't going to be a slut like some of the other girls. I started getting angry, but I never lashed out at him. Instead, I walked away and went straight to Malik's house.

As we headed for the basement, I could hear his/our friends talking. I stopped right on the steps, pulled him in for a kiss and placed my hand on the front of his jeans. He pulled away, ran down the rest of the steps and kicked them out. That evening was the first time I felt lips on my breast and got fingered. When I returned home, Lawrence was sitting out in the yard at TT's waiting on my return. He was heated that I walked away from him and made me sit next to him as he talked to me about my behavior. Although I wasn't listening to him, his devotion to waiting for me made me feel special and loved. He promised he would come and see me the next day and he did!

I avoided going over to Malik's for a few days because my father was acting like a caring dad. I reveled in the attention. He took me over to Julia's and stayed with us. He even cooked! I was happy and overjoyed. When he brought me home, he told me that he would see me again after visiting with TT. After a few hours, I went to TT's looking for him. When she informed me that he left a while ago, I was hurt. He didn't even come to say goodbye.

I left TT's and went straight to Maliks' where he put on a porno to show me how to perform oral sex.

Walking back home, a sadness came over me that I didn't understand. I had no energy to fight with my sister or be rude to my mother. I just wanted to be left alone. I wanted a new family in a different state.

One morning as I was ironing a shirt for church, I picked up the iron and held it close to my face. Wondering what would happen if I went to church with this burn across my face. Feeling the steam and questioning if my mom would go to jail? Would I end up in foster care? I then looked at the mark on my arm from accidentally burning myself and recalled the pain. Upon deciding that I didn't want to feel that pain on my face, I went back to ironing and thinking of ways to get out of my life.

Running away wasn't an option. My mom always told us if we were to ever run away, we could only wear and take anything that we purchased. Being only twelve, I didn't own anything that I purchased so running away naked was not up for consideration. *Side Note: I ran away when I was five.. I had my clothes on and a bookbag with some toys. I might have been successful had I not left my mom a note telling her "I will be at TT's so don't look for me."*

After days passed of ignoring Malik, he came on my block looking for me. When I told him that I hated my life, he asked if I thought about my life when I was fooling around with him? "No. The only thoughts I had was how much fun I was having and how good it felt." It dawned on me that when I was fooling around, no one or nothing else mattered. Not Lawrence or my mom. The next day, I was back in his basement.

With as many times I hung out with him, I soon realized that the euphoria would only last so long before I needed him again. We were both virgins and wanted to keep it that way, so nothing more than the tip was ever allowed in. We had enough fun without engaging in full penetration. This went on until I turned thirteen and started fooling around with other guys from around the way who were older than me. I would either let them finger me or give me oral. I didn't return the oral because I wasn't keen on putting various penises in my mouth.

Each time I was with someone, the fun was only in the activity. Once things were over, I had to focus on it to keep it in the forefront of my mind to keep the negative thoughts away that brought on the sadness. A destructive cycle I didn't realize I was in. This went on until I met Derrick.

Oh! He Cute

Derrick became my world. He was on the basketball team, and I was a cheerleader. After one game, I sent my friend over to him to find out if he liked me and he did. I fell head over heels in love with him. Fooling around with Malik stopped. I didn't want anyone else in my life but him.

It was the middle of ninth grade when I found out that another one of my good friends Yanez had sex with Derrick. It was my tipping point. Especially since he and I had only gotten so far as kissing, and I let all the other guys go. The hurt and betrayal I felt, combined with the sadness of constantly being an option for my father, mixed with low self-esteem, did not result in a perfect outcome. Exhaustion from keeping everything inside became too much to handle.

I took all the available pills around the house and went to lay in my mother's bed while she was out, and Regina was cleaning the kitchen. I thought that it would serve her right to find me dead in her bed. However, God had a different plan. He made me get up and go to the kitchen. For what, who knows. Regina thought I was drunk and called TT over to get me in trouble.

When I recently asked my mother what she remembers of this night, her response "It's a night I will never forget. The doctor that took care of you got reprimanded for doing so." She asked my sister, and her response was "I recall her laying on your bed talking about purple elephants." That's all they remember from that night. Either way, my mom came home and took me to the hospital.

There, I can see bits and pieces, like the nurse who is trying to get me to drink a cup of charcoal to counteract the number of pills I took. I remember spitting out the rancid black liquid only to be told if I didn't drink it, they would have to put a tube in either in my nose or mouth that would go down my esophagus. Despite the nastiness of it, I drunk, gagged and swallowed the liquid that tasted like thick barely cooked grits with no seasoning. Ironically, I was more afraid of the tube than dying.

A night's stay in the hospital included a trip to the Psych ward for evaluation. This was to determine if I needed an extended stay, or if I could get released. Exiting the elevator, we (my mom and I) had to wait in this ugly mint green room that had bars on the windows. Looking at the world past the bars was nothing new. The back of our apartment had two windows that were right in front of the fire escape. I knew how to look past the bars to see outside so that didn't bother me. What bothered me was the quietness.

It was eerily quiet with a stillness in the air that was broken only by occasional movements and murmurs, which seemed more like background sounds. What scared me immensely was the suggestion that I may need to stay there. WHAT? I saw the movie *Reform School Girls*. That movie instilled in me the fear of being institutionalized. I did not want to be raped by other inmates or tortured by any guards. I prayed frantically for God to not keep me there. Prayed that He would speak for me, so I could go home.

The next day, my prayer answered as my mom took me home with the requirement of seeing a mental health professional as an outpatient. Coming home, I felt dead inside. Lawrence was at TT's waiting on my arrival. Sitting on the sofa, Lawrence sat next to me because he wanted to see about his 'baby girl" and spoke of how much he loved me. The only problem was that it didn't feel genuine. It felt more like an obligation because people were around. My pastor, mom, Papa and TT, so of course he had to play the role of doting father. However, he didn't stay long. I wasn't in the mood for his fake concern anyway. Nor did I feel the need to explain my choice to anyone. If I choose to die, it was my life to take. Right? Of course, I know better now, but then, I was a teenager caught up in my own drama not knowing how to seek help.

Lawrence came by a few more times, then did his same old talk of coming through and not showing up. After removing his attention from me, I decided that he wasn't worth the time. If I saw him on the block, I would say hello and keep it moving. No longer would I seek his love and attention. Yes. I was still hurt. I was, at the time, his only child. *Rumor has it that I may have an older sibling somewhere.* I pushed the hurt aside and told myself not to care. Not caring was easy to do when I didn't see him. The days that I did see him were when I would have conversations with myself about why he no longer mattered.

I was still longing for something, and you know the saying, "when you look for something, you are going to find it."

Faulty Anticipation

A few months passed, and life became normal again. The attempt to end my life seemed like someone else's story. I only saw a therapist twice because my mom couldn't find someone she thought was suitable for me. The one I did see was young and kept irritating me by flipping her hair in front then behind her ear. Church, school and dance classes were a good distraction, except when I was alone. By myself, my thoughts became too much to handle. Hanging out with my friends wasn't enough. I needed something that would quiet the voices in my head.

Voices that told me I was a failure. Couldn't even end my life correctly. That I was ugly. No one could ever love me. That my existence made my mother regret not having an abortion. Usually, when I got tired of all the inner conflict, I'd read or call one of the guys I fooled around with before cutting them off for Derrick.

But even with all of that, there was an unsatisfied piece of me. This piece held the intense sadness where I just wanted to be left alone. I made the decision to forgive Derrick because of the friendship he showed to me in the weeks following my attempt. Yanez on the other hand, I wanted nothing to do with. Our friendship became strained. *Side note: Why do some females do that? Lose the girlfriend but keep the guy when they both betrayed you?*

One day, Derrick and I skipped school to hang out at his house. There, I gave him my virginity. It was not what I expected. He fell asleep right after he came. As I felt his condom covered penis slide out, I laid there not knowing what to do. Do I wake him up? Is this normal? What is wrong with me? Did he really go to sleep? Am I that bad? After what felt like a long time but was only a minute or two, I shook him awake, and he unsuccessfully tried to have a go at it again. I decided to leave.

Sitting on the L train going home, thoughts of him falling asleep consumed me that I couldn't focus on the actual intercourse. I sat talking to God. "I know what I just did was sinful, but what in heaven's name just happened? Like. I know I came twice and wanted more but how does one fall asleep? I'm sorry Father 'cause I'm sure you don't want to hear this." With my 15th birthday being the next day, I realized I gave Derrick a better gift than he gave me.

I decided to clear my head by taking a longer walk home. I got off at Myrtle and Broadway, went to McDonalds to give my girlfriend a quick update and get some free fries. After kicking it with her, I started to feel a little better. Outside of the McDonalds, there were some guys hanging out and one guy was dribbling a basketball. As I passed by them, one of the guys started hollering at me which I ignored. Still caught in my thoughts and all. About mid-way the block, I heard someone bouncing a ball behind me and sidestepped so they could pass. Instead of walking past, he started walking next to me asking me not to give him the shoulder.

He introduced himself as Calvin and wanted to know if I lived in the area. Getting a good look at him, I liked what I saw. Dark skin guy with a black flight jacket over a hoodie and long gym shorts and a low ceaser (haircut). I told him my cross streets, and he did the same. He then asked if he could walk me home since we lived close to each other. I let him know he could go as far as my corner but not to my house. That was fine with him. When we got to my corner, we exchanged numbers.

The next morning, Calvin called me before I left for school to wish me a Happy Birthday and to see if I'd be able to see him later. I said I would meet him at McDonalds, and he could walk me home. *I introduced him to the block to keep him safe.* We spoke more about ourselves and realized we had a lot in common. Both of us were being raised by our mothers and our fathers were not around. We both had an older sister and enjoyed being with our grandparents. I enjoyed talking with him that we kept right on to my house. After a short conversation in the hallway, he left telling me he would call me later.

"Did you get any mail today?"
"Nope. I got a card yesterday but not today."
"Are you sure you got all the mail?"
"Yes, I'm sure. Why?"
"I think you should check your mailbox again." He says with humor in his voice.
"Why would I check it again? The mail doesn't come twice."
"I really think you need to check your mailbox again."
"Oh, my goodness! Will you stop talking about the mail? I'll check it just to get you to stop asking. Do you want to hold or me call you back?"
"I'll wait."

I quickly go down the steps and as I reach the bottom, I see a card and a red rose on the floor. I run back up the stairs.

"Aww Calvin! That is so sweet. Thank you."
"I mean what I say inside. Go read it and I'll see you tomorrow."

I hung up and opened the card. On the inside was a simple Happy Birthday. Underneath that, he wrote: "LaChelle. I believe we are going to be together for a long time. Happy Birthday." That was the first of many times Calvin was my personal mailman.

A month after being hot and heavy with kissing and dry humping, we had sex with me letting him believe he was getting my virginity. *What? Did you think after that mess with Derrick I wasn't going to take my status back?* Plus, Derrick wanted nothing more to do with me. When I tried to meet up with him again for a do-over, he was never available. Soon after, no one was able to reach him. Rumors had it that he was either living in Puerto Rico, Virginia or dead from a shooting he was involved in.

Once Calvin and I had sex, we always had sex. Whether it was our bedrooms, at his friends, or in the hallway if my mom was home. One time we got caught by his mom and I froze in fear. She said, "Calvin, you have to tell me when you have her over," and stepped back out. We jumped out the bed, dressed and went out to talk to his mom. She asked us if we were using protection. We told her we were, and she said, "Ok" and left it at that. I was surprised at her calmness. When my mom caught me with a guy on the sofa with his hands in my pants, he got kicked out and I got lectures, scriptures and prayers. Long, long prayers.

Six months later, we were in love and happy, or so I thought. I was crushed when I found out he was cheating on me. I broke it off and spent days crying. One day I got tired of crying and him apologizing, that I went over to Malik's. It was summer so we just sat on the stoop talking. This guy that lived across the street from him would flirt with me on occasion and he didn't know I had a crush on him for a long time. When Malik said he was going in to eat, I headed across the street.

"How old are you?" I asked being that he was outside with no one around him which was rare.
"Why do you want to know."
"Because. I'm tired of having a crush on you."
"Aren't you Lawrence's daughter?"
"Yeah. What about it?"
"Well. I know him and he's a good guy."
Getting a little irritated I said "I don't want to talk about Lawrence. I've had a crush on you for years and I want to know what it would be like to be with you?"
"How old are you?"
"Fifteen."
"We can't be seen together." He says as he's looking me over.

"I know. I just want to get with you and make my daydreams come true."
"You mean you want to tell all your friends, and it get back to your family and get me in trouble? Mess up my home?"
"Absolutely not. I want this experience with you to be mine and known by me, you and God."
"Meet me at the bus stop at Halsey and Evergreen. I'll pick you up there and we can go somewhere."

That somewhere was a cemetery in Queens not too far from where we lived. It was dark, making the cemetery even spookier than it already is. Driving deep into the cemetery, my heart was racing. Part in anticipation that I was finally going to be with my crush, and part the location. He positioned the seats to make it comfortable and put a condom on. I felt disappointed because the ease of his movements let me know he did this all the time, and I was just another chick.

While he fucked me in the back of his jeep, all I could think about were the souls that were watching us. What were they thinking of my actions? I didn't feel special, and the intercourse didn't blow my mind. I thought for a twenty-four-year-old, he would be better than the guys my age. But it was a forgettable experience. When he was done, we exchanged casual conversations on the way home. He wanted me to understand how no one could know about this because he had a family. I assured him that this was my choice and had no intention of bragging. I told him that I also need his word he wouldn't say anything. We agreed it would be our secret.

He then wanted to give me insight on father/daughter relationships. I was thinking *nigga please shut up and drop me off*. I started to say just that as he kept on talking. When he dropped me off at the same spot he picked me up from, I was irritable and frustrated. Walking home, I disliked myself. Questioning how fulfilling your desire with someone you fantasized about could leave you feeling pissed. The disgust for myself was overwhelming, so when I returned home and found out Calvin called, I called him back. It had been a few weeks since we broke up. He asked if he could come over for a little while and I said yes. When he came, he was full of apologies and told me he wanted to get back together. Because I loved him more than I loved myself, I took him back.

We would break up three more times before we got to twelfth grade. Each of these break-ups were due to his cheating. After each breakup, I would start messing with other guys.

Our last breakup was the longest, one month. In that month, I started seeing someone I liked and played the good virgin so he wouldn't push moving past a kiss on the lips. When Calvin found out, he was not happy. He broke it off with the girl he was with and worked on getting me back through and notes from my personal mailman. It worked. He really was the only guy I wanted and loved. He was liked by my family as I was by his.

We understood each other. Neither of us were ashamed to cry to each other. We were each other's safe space. Accepting all our flaws without judgement. Calvin and I fit as if we were made for each other. He just had a hard time not seeing other girls.

Snow on the Ground

Friend: I typed this chapter once. My editor made suggestions and as I tried to make the corrections, I just couldn't. After I write the words *God I hate this chapter*, I decided to write this note instead. Fighting tears. I can't do it. So, I apologize for any errors after that line. I very rarely go back to this night. Please forgive any errors.

In January of '94, I had met this guy named Juice that also lived in the area. After a few phone conversations with him, he invited me to his house. It was snowing, and a few inches were already on the ground. I had just gotten off the phone with Calvin who broke off our date for his "friends." I told him that I was going over to this guy's house to hang out and that he could page me if he wanted to see me.

As I walked through the snow to Juice's house, I had a bad feeling, but I put it out of my mind. I told myself I was just going to stay for an hour then get back home.

When I arrived at his house, he took me to his room in the basement. There we talked while music played in the background. He showed me his book of sketches. After looking at them and talking with him, I realized I didn't like him enough to stay there. When I told him I was going to go, he didn't want me to leave and asked if I could dance with him to this song that had just started playing. It was a good song. I laughed and told him, "Only one dance then I'm leaving. It's snowing pretty heavily, and I don't want to walk through too much snow."

He agreed, and we danced. I believe it was a reggae song. When I went to pick up my coat, he snatched it and threw it out of his room and closed the door. I walked to the door ready to leave and not finding his action funny. He blocked me as I approached the door.

"How you gonna dance with me and then leave?"
"Why did you throw my coat?"
"Because. You can't dance with me and then leave. You got me rock hard." He grabs himself and I notice how his penis is alert.

"Listen, I'm sorry. If I knew you were going to react like this, I wouldn't have given you the dance now please move aside."
"No. You can't go and leave me like this. Don't you know dancing is nothing but foreplay? You got me hard. And you are going to do something about it."

I try to get around him thinking that I wasn't even grinding on him like that. He pushes me away from the door and then once more landing me on his bed.

I start to get up, but he pushes me back down.

I try to make a run for it, but the room is small he gets to me before I can make it to the door. He is angry and pushes me harder towards the bed. "Bitch! I said we are going to take care of this." He has me pinned. I can't recall exactly how he had me pinned. He starts to unbuckle his belt with the free arm that is not being used to assist me in staying down.

I remember that I heard somewhere that if your attacker is angry, don't fight back because he can turn violent and may kill you. *God I hate this chapter.*

I think *no one knows where I am. They only knew I was going to a new friend's house named Juice.* As he proceeds to pull his penis out, I whisper, "If you must do this, please use a condom." His response was, "Shut the fuck up bitch and don't even bother about trying to scream. No one else is down here." Those were the last words I heard.

That thing I remember was being in the dark. My mind was in a dark place. It was dark, not only because I closed my eyes, but because that is where I went. I went into the darkness. I felt nothing in the darkness. I don't know how long I was there. When I came out of the darkness, I was walking in the snow with my coat open and tears running down my face. As I got to the corner of my block, I saw Lawrence. He told me to close my coat, then asked why I was crying. I looked at him and from a place of nothingness I said, "He raped me. I wanted to leave but he wouldn't let me go. He raped me." He told me to go home and resumed walking. I watched him walk away down the block and was back in the darkness. I saw TT at her door when I came home. She said she had a bad feeling about me. I just looked at her and went inside our apartment.

It is funny what the mind remembers and what it doesn't. I can remember the conversation with Lawrence and him walking away. I can remember TT. Yet I don't remember how my mother found out.

Recently, I found the courage to ask my mom how the cops came because I can't recall. She stated that I came inside crying and saying "he raped me" repeatedly. No one, not my mom, sister or older cousin could get me to tell them his name. She called the cops, and I wouldn't even tell them.

I am fighting off a panic attack right now. My head hurts and I am nauseous. Mainly because this is the first time I have allowed myself to fully and purposely go back there. I don't like going to this night.

Out of the darkness, I find myself on a hospital bed with my legs in stirrups as the doctor is taking a swab of my vaginal wall for a rape kit. I hear her say, "There is some abrasion, but I don't see enough evidence of force."

To that I quietly say "ever since I started my menstrual, I am always moist down there. Sometimes there is so much discharge that I must change my underwear so no; my body made it easy for him to enter although I didn't want him to."
"Well, that will explain why we won't get anything from this swab," she tells someone I cannot see.

I am asked if I am pressing charges. I think about what I just heard from the doctor. I know no Judge will believe I was raped because there isn't enough damage done to my vaginal area that will show the sex was not wanted. Because my body worked against me, no one will believe me. They will say I wanted it. They will say that going over to his home was done with the intent to have sex. They will say I asked for it. With tears running down my face from the thoughts of how they will make it seem that I am lying. That I wanted him. I quietly answer, "No." I am back in the darkness.

The next time I come to myself, Calvin is standing in front of me asking where does this guy live? I tell him I don't remember, and he shows me the gun in his pants and tells me he is ready to take care of him. Rage is in his eyes as he pleads with me to remember. I begin crying telling him I don't. I was more concerned with him going to jail than exacting revenge. It was too soon. He would make the perfect suspect. I refused to give him what information I could remember, which was nothing but a name and that would be enough for him. When he left, I went back into the darkness.

I reside in the darkness for a few days. When I finally come back to myself, it is with the determination that I will not live life like a victim. I decided in clarity, that this will not define or defeat me. It will be categorized as sex without permission. Matter fact, I won't count it at all. It is my senior year. I have senior prom and graduation to look towards. I will not let him take these moments away from me. I say all this to myself looking in a mirror as the water running for my bath helps to buffer my cries. I repeat everything several times until the tears stop. When they do, I tell myself that that was the last cry I will have for this. I will not give this event anymore tears. I get in my bath and softly sing I Surrender All.

I surrender all.
All to thee my blessed Savior
I surrender all.

It's only the chorus but I sing it repeatedly until my water goes cold. I stand and declare to God that I am surrendering this to him. I will not carry it with me to the point that it keeps me from living. The request and offering of something to drink using the word juice was starting to make me freeze and give me anxiety. I did not want to continue living with that. I had to let it go.

It would not be until March that Calvin calls me again. I haven't spoken to him since that night he was at my house with his gun. I welcome him back. He tells me he was angry with me and needed space. I tell him I never want to talk about it again and ask him not to bring it up. We get back together taking things slowly. He spent a lot of time just holding me and we fell deeper in love. It wouldn't be until the night of my prom in May, that I was able to once again have sex. . *Thank God camera phones were not a thing in 1994.*

The prom was at one Pier 17 down at South Street Seaport. It was that night that Calvin got down on one knee and said, "LaChelle. I don't have a ring to give you, but I have given you my heart. I am asking you to be mine forever. Will you marry me?" To which I replied, "YES!" I was ecstatic.

I loved Calvin and wanted to be his wife. With me leaving for college in August, we spent all the time we could together. One night, my mom went away, and with my sister was already away at college, he came and spent the night. It wasn't the first time we spent the night together; it was just the first time at my house, and I was sick with a cold. While we were in bed, TT knocked on the door to check on me. He hid in the back room as I received soup and love from her. When she left, he came back out. We were very close to getting caught, and it turned us on. Although I was sick, we made love in a way we never did before. I sweated so much that I woke up feeling better. That night was so special. Not only for the time we took loving each other, it was also the night we conceived.

Time to Choose

For as long as I can remember, my mom had always told my sister and I that she would not pay for us to attend college if we were to get pregnant. The logic was that if we felt we were mature enough to bring a baby into the world, then we could use that same mentality to find a job and take care of that child. We could also take care of our own education.

I realized I missed my period after a week of not being able to keep anything down and feeling tired all the time. I asked Calvin for twenty dollars and went to a drugstore to buy a home pregnancy test. Not believing the results, we went to a free clinic in the Village for a professional urinalysis test. With a positive result in my pocket, I became aware that a choice would have to be made. A choice made harder by Calvin who was excited with the prospect of being a dad.

At the time I found out I was pregnant; my room was stocked with things for my dorm. The trunk had sheets, towels, bath supplies and other things you need to live away from home. I was nervous, excited and saddened to be going away. I'd just graduated from high school in the top twenty-five of the last graduating class and with the second highest GPA in Accounting. I couldn't wait to see what I could accomplish in college. I had a Presidential Scholarship and was on my way to the University to get my degree in accounting.

Investments into my future had already been made. Loans had already been taken out. Purchases were sitting in my room. Expectations of a college student were not lost. My mom took me to the doctor to have another test done to confirm the pregnancy. When it came back that I was, she showed no emotion. She reminded me of where she stood, and the decision would be mine alone. I had a choice to make. But then, not really. I knew the way she expected me to go. How? Because, with the ultimatum known, she was still making purchases for my education out of state.

When I told Calvin that I wanted to go to college and that it wouldn't be an option if I had it, he started thinking of ways I could still go to school. We could both find work, stay at his grandparents', get married and after the baby was born, I could focus on attending a city university. It sounded good, but it wasn't the path I wanted to take.

My mom was planning for her child to go away. I wanted to go away. There was nothing to discuss. Calvin was trying to convince me to stay, and his mom gave the pregnancy her blessing. Don't get me wrong, she wasn't happy about it, but she was going to support him if fatherhood was what he chose. When it came time for me to leave for school, he came over to the house asking me not to go. He knew what it meant for the pregnancy if I left.

I was still experiencing horrible all-day sickness at school. Trying to cover it up from my three roommates was easy since it was early in the pregnancy, and I wasn't showing. I blamed the nausea on being away from home and they bought it. The first week of school, on a Thursday night, there was a late-night event that the basketball team was putting on. Buses were running to take students there and back. On the way there, something surreal, *at least in my opinion,* happened. Club Nouveau's version of *Lean on Me* started playing on the radio and someone asked the bus driver to turn it up. When he did everyone started singing.

It was like a musical out of a movie. It was a popular song and almost everyone knew the words and sang along. The end of the song had all the girls singing *Call Me* and all the guys singing the response part. The experience filled my soul and at that moment,

I realized that I was no longer at home, but a student pursuing my higher education.

On the bus heading back to the dorms, there was no singing, but there was excitement of a different kind.

I was wracked with severe stomach pains. Every pain caused me to double over. I was sweating profusely, and my pulse was racing. The pain was intense. I thought I was having a miscarriage. I was feeling a lot of wetness between my legs. I had to go to a hospital, and to do that, I had to tell someone my secret. I told the girl next to me who then told the driver who drove to the nearest hospital.

An upperclassman got off the bus with me to escort me in and stay with me so the bus could return to campus. When they called me into the room, he came along. They assumed he was the father and allowed him in. They did a sonogram and showed me the little pea sized fetus that had a heartbeat. It was healthy and fast. The doctor told me what I was experiencing was not a miscarriage, but a bad case of gas. GAS! How embarrassing! My secret was revealed all due to gas! A secret that was being removed from my body the following week. All was not well!

I called Calvin when I returned to my empty dorm room. He told me it was a sign that I shouldn't go through with the termination. I cried telling him I had no choice. The singing on the bus made me feel that I was right where I was supposed to be. I was in tears when he hung up on me. The next day was filled with worry about the number of people who now knew that there was a pregnant freshman on campus.

I heard whispers and saw side glances. Felt eyes with laser focus rays and heard everyone talking about the pregnant freshman.

Except, that wasn't happening at all. People weren't gawking or talking, and if they were, I didn't hear it. I decided to put all my attention into my studies. Later that day though, I received a package from my personal mailman. It was a cassette tape of the song *Endless Love* by Luther Vandross and Mariah Carey. I cried as I listened to it the rest of the night and the following days.

On Thursday, a week after the gas fiasco, I was on the bus heading home to get ready for Saturday. That Friday, I spent the day with Calvin. He told me he had a dream that I was carrying a girl. We picked out a name for her, Tiara Ariel. We tried to have sex, but we were both too emotional. Neither one of us wanted the decision I made. As I lay against him, he was rubbing my belly asking me not to get rid of his baby. His daughter. As time passed, we wondered who Tiara would look like. What kind of parents would we be? We daydreamed about our life together as three. It was unhealthy to do, but deep down, I wanted her.

On Saturday, Calvin did not go with us. Arriving at the clinic, there were protesters with signs standing on either side of the building as close to the door as they were allowed. Police officers were there to make sure they stayed behind the barricade. Not only were there signs saying abortion is murder or every fetus is a life, but there were also signs with visuals of bleeding and dismembered infants.

At first sighting of them, my chest tightened, and fear came over me. I would say doubt but that never left. As my mom and I proceeded to cross the street to get into the clinic, anger replaced fear. As we got closer, their shouts got louder. People reaching out to hand me pamphlets letting me know I had other options.

I wanted to turn and yell at them. Let them know that all their protesting was not going to change my situation. Their pamphlets were not going to give me money to go to school and raise this baby if I had it. That what I am dislodging from my body is a fetus and not an infant that would be able to live for one day if I had it now. Stepping into the elevator, I was still angry. I wanted to go back and tell them everything I was thinking. To ask them if they are the same people who would get mad at another young black girl from the ghetto who would need welfare because she got knocked up? I wanted someone to agree with that just so I could correct them and let them know I didn't live in the ghetto, and my mom was college educated and wanted that for me. That my mother always said that God gives us free-will and is a forgiving God. So be like Jesus and forgive me and move on. Instead, the elevator doors opened and the mental fight with the protestors ceased.

I was entering a last chance space.

The last opportunity to run and become a mom at seventeen.

We checked in and settled down to fill out paperwork. My mom sat next to me silently reading a book. Very little was said. When I asked what would happen if I didn't go through with it. Her response was one question. "Are you ready to get a job and pay me back the money spent?" Nothing more was said. It didn't need to be. I sat waiting in my own thoughts until my name was called. I got the anesthesia because I did not want to feel anything. I was already feeling enough.

That night, Calvin called and asked me to come outside in ten minutes. When the time was up, I looked out the window to see if he was downstairs. There he was sitting on his bike holding on to the gate as if he stopped to speak to someone. Outside, that someone was me. He never got off the bike when he saw me. "Did you go through with it?" I looked at him with tears running down and quietly said yes. He didn't say anything. He only rode off. I watched him until I couldn't see him. In that moment, I decided that I would never have another abortion. NO MATTER WHAT!

My roommates did end up finding out I was pregnant due to the morning sickness that lasted all day and was hard to continue hiding. I'm sure the coincidence of going home for a weekend and returning no longer pregnant was not lost on anyone. However, since we were all still getting to know each other, the subject didn't come up. A few days later, my roommate across from me had her boyfriend over.

He was playing by drawing on her board with a marker stuck between his toes. What he drew resembled a fetus in its sac. I stopped laughing and started crying. She sat up to look at what it was and immediately erased it and slapped his foot. She whispered to him what he drew, and he became very apologetic.

In that moment, I became fully aware of what I had done. I cried. My heart raced. I became very sweaty and started hyperventilating. Dizziness and light-headedness washed over me, and I passed out right there on my bed. When I came to, there was a cold cloth on my forehead, and a banana and orange juice on my nightstand. I called Calvin and he told me that I had made the decision and now I had to live with it.

He broke up with me a few days later.

Higher Education

The sadness and need to seclude myself along with thoughts of suicide returned. It didn't help that some of my classes proved to be a little difficult. I was depressed. Going through the motions of being a student and thinking if I should just end my life. A life that I didn't feel was worth living. Then somebody showed up in my dorm.

Nicole. *My friend that lived across the street from Malik.*

The cloud was lifted. We became inseparable. We were seen so much together, that when we weren't, the question always asked was, "Where is your partner in crime?" And because Calvin and I were no longer together, there was no reason to go home every weekend. We hit all the parties and after parties and after-after parties.

The part of me that was still depressed and in need of an emotional escape found freedom in college. It came in the forms of freshman and upperclassmen. Guys on campus and off. It was happy with alcohol in my system. I told myself that I will enjoy the freedom of not being home, enjoy the ability of doing what I want when I wanted. I will allow myself to enjoy all of this if my grades did not show a lack of focus. I will not go into the many things I did for two reasons. One, I would like to get married again, and two, it truly would need to be a whole other book. Either way, it's too many stories and not enough space. Also, it is not what *this* book is about. I will tell you one story though.

It was an after-after party located at an off-campus house after one of the fraternity's step shows. Nothing but good music and a steady supply of alcohol. The party was on the third floor because it was void of any furniture. The liquor was red grain alcohol. It tasted and looked like Cherry Kool-Aid. It was sweet, fruity and had you going back for more. *This is where I always ask myself what the hell was I thinking?*

The alcohol was in the tub of the bathroom. If you needed to use the restroom, you had to go to the second floor. This would have been fine, but expecting a bunch of drunk college kids to follow the rules of the party was a bit much. I can remember that the bathroom door on the third floor was closed several times. Thinking of the types of liquid that tub received, especially since it was always full sends shivers down my spine. I just hope the alcohol disinfected the urine and God knows what else.

Drinking as much as I did gave me a hangover for three days. The first day I was still drunk. The last two were spent nursing a hangover. Looking back, I probably had a mild case of alcohol poisoning. Nevertheless, the lesson was received, and I never did that again.

During all this partying, I started to miss church. I knew what I was doing couldn't be healthy, but I thought because I had an abortion, I could not enter His house. However, the yearning to be in church wouldn't let up. I found a Baptist church and attended. By the time I sat down and looked around, I noticed I was the only one of me there. It would be rude to walk out. Plus, I needed the comfort that only church provides. After all, isn't church the hospital for broken people? There was no screaming from the pulpit nor were the songs accompanied by the beats of a drum. It was a quiet service. Something I wasn't used to. When I left, my soul was not fed. I went home the next week just to attend service.

On my eighteenth birthday, I found myself focusing on my non-existent relationship with Lawrence and how it impacted me.

At the end of the evening when dinner was on last call, I left the cafeteria to walk around campus and think. I walked the campus and surrounding area for two hours. By the third hour, I was angry and called TT for Lawrence's number. When he answered, I asked him to listen and not speak. I laid it on him. I told him he was the reason I became promiscuous at a young age. That what I was seeking and needing from him, I found in boys and men, when I should have still been playing hopscotch and double-dutch. I went from yelling to crying back to yelling again for about forty minutes.

He never said a word. If he did, I couldn't hear through my anger. Whatever I was holding on my chest for as many years I can remember came out that night. When I was done, I asked:

"Why couldn't you love me?"
"Are you done?"
"Yes"
"Good."
"Are you going to answer my question?"
"No."
"Ok then. From this moment on, I don't have a father. You will forever just be Lawrence to me."
"I am your father, and you will call me such."
"No. I am good. I think I'm going to be ok. Bye."

But I wasn't okay. Far from it.

With the conversation over, the emotions I was feeling was too much to bear and I found myself releasing them in the bed of an Alpha man. While my PIC released her pain with his line brother at the other end of the room.

I started slowing down when she didn't return sophomore year. Started having actual relationships instead of one-night stands, long weekends and mid-week fun. Through one of these relationships, I met Asha. To this day, she is one of my closest friends. Thanks to honesty, love, non-judgement and respect. Even when we get upset with each other, it's only from hearing the truth. It's because of that truth; we keep coming back to our table of friendship. We vent to each other about everything and encourage each other with the same love and respect. She is my soulmate.

During this sophomore year, I also met Xavier and Jason. Xavier at school, and Jason coming off Greyhound one weekend when I came home. They were both on and off again relationships. In between them, I continued to have fun at a slower pace. I started seeing a guy I would see around campus.

We started talking and the first time I went to his house we had sex. Because I was doing so many, condoms were an important part of my life, and I liked to watch them put it on. When he flipped me over so that I was on my stomach, and said he was coming, I reached around to grab the top of the condom, and it wasn't there.

I asked where it was, and he said, "I took it off to come, don't worry I'll shoot it on your back." I moved from under him and told him that I did not give permission for him to remove the condom. I gathered my clothes, peed on his front porch and left. *I'd like to stop and thank God for the lack of camera phones during this era.* This incident, however, made me slow down even more after my STD test came back positive for Chlamydia.

Junior year came around and the only guys I messed with on a consistent basis were Xavier and Jason. Xavier was for school and Jason was my consistent when I was back in Brooklyn. With both guys, I had back-ups for if they weren't available to satisfy my need. Because that was what sex was for me. The way to calm the mental bouncing off the walls and keep my sanity.

When Xavier wanted to stop using condoms. I informed him we needed to be careful because an abortion was NOT an option.

Been there, done that and suffered for it. I stopped seeing everyone once we took our relationship deeper. It was easy to do as he had no problem catering to my needs. We conceived our son prior to the April Fool's Day blizzard of '97.

When I told my family, I told them my plan. I would attend summer school to graduate a trimester early. This meant that I would be finished with school in February instead of May. I would pump during the week freezing the milk and bringing it home with me every weekend. This plan left little questions to be asked. It was a solid plan.

My mother, fine with this pregnancy because it came as I was graduating, had only one concern. If I would have enough time to bond. I said that I can take a week out of school without penalty. TT said she already knew what I was going to tell her; she just wanted to hear my plans. *My grandmother had a little second sight and passed it on to me.* I received her approval, and she touched my belly stating that this baby was going to be extremely smart since it will be attending college while developing.

Our son Kamar was born that November. When February came, it proved that I stuck to my plan to be back home with my son a trimester early. I graduated with a degree in Accounting and a Concentration in Psychology and made the Dean's List.

After several years of messing with Jason off and on, we got pregnant in 2002. That is the last time I saw him. He decided that fatherhood wasn't something he wanted and stopped all contact with me. When I went looking for him at his mother's, she told me something that I've never forgotten. "Jason ain't worth the shit flies land on." Whoa! I would never describe Autumn's father to her like that. *She now knows this story.*

During my pregnancy, I found out that Calvin had moved to the South and was murdered there. When my daughter was born, I gave her Calvin's middle name.

I loved being a mom of two. Even if I was doing it partially on my own. Kamar's dad and I called it off during the pregnancy, but he would come and get him every other weekend. My kids were everything to me and Autumn was everything to Kamar. You had to get his permission to hold her or play with her. He was her little protector, and he was my handsome, funny little boy with an intelligence that surpassed his years.

BOOK TWO

Love at First Sight

Spring in New York is my favorite time of the year. It's cool enough to wear a jacket or sweatshirt. The streets are full of people going about their business or just enjoying the weather. The stoops are full of friends and family talking smack or of serious issues. And the air is full of the beauty of the city, which are all the different cultures that inhabit this concrete jungle. It was a lovely Spring Day in April when I found myself Downtown Brooklyn to get the kids some summer clothes.

I bumped into this man outside of Cookies and when I looked into his eyes, I froze for a second. His eyes were deep brown with a hint of green in them. He asked if I was ok and I apologized for not looking where I was going. We moved out each other's way and as I headed for the entrance of Cookies, I couldn't help but look back. When I did, we locked eyes again. As I picked out things for my babies to wear, I thought no more about him.

It wasn't until I was waiting for the B26 in front of the Jay Street – Borough Hall train station that I started thinking about him. Mentally kicking myself for not speaking with him as I most likely will never get another opportunity. Or so I thought. Standing at the bus stop not sucking on a lollipop (LL Cool J's *Around the Way Girl* reference), someone lightly pulled on my jacket. As I turned around, I found myself staring at the man from earlier. Quickly taking in his dirty bomber jacket, dusty shirt, jeans and construction boots, the first thought that came to mind was *this is my husband*.

"Why you lookin' all mean?" he asks.
"If I was just standing here smiling for no reason, you'd think I was crazy." I reply with a little flirtation in my tone.
"Naw. I'd just think that you thinkin' of your man and he putting that smile on your face."

"Nope. Only my kids put a smile on my face but right now it's you."

"Oh, you got game." He says while he adjusts the hard hat that is hanging on the strap of a bag that's across his chest.

"No game. Just facts but my bus is here, and I must say I am glad I got to see you again."

"You gonna see me again on my word. I'm Nathan and whose name should I put next to this number you about to give me?"

He called me that night and we talked every day for a week. By the time the weekend came around, with Kamar at his dad's, I dropped Autumn off with my mom and had him over for dinner. We ate. We fucked and I fell in love. Within a few short weeks, TT was calling him her grandson-in-law, Kamar played ball with him, and he became like a dad to Autumn minus changing or bathing her. *I'm not crazy.*

Because he worked construction and would leave early in the morning around four and didn't always want to wake me up to lock the door, he was given a key. During the week, he would stop by after work, then go home to change, get his work clothes and return for the overnight stay.

On the weekends, he'd spend a few hours during the day then home which was the way I liked it. Weekends when Kamar stayed home, that was our time to be our family of three and enjoy all that New York has to offer. By June, he picked up more hours on the job but still made time every day to spend with us. He even tried to stay over at least several nights during the week.

We moved this way until the night of July 3rd when someone started calling my number and hanging up once I answered. They did this every hour and since Kamar was with his dad, I couldn't shut the phone off. When Nathan came, I informed him that someone thought it funny to keep calling and not saying anything. He took the phone and waited. It didn't take long to ring again.

"Whoever the fuck this is, stop calling this number." He says with such venom you would have thought it was his number being harassed. As he flips the phone closed, he advises me to turn it off.

"I can't. I'm waiting on Xavier to call me to let me know when he's bringing Kamar home." I look at him studying his face to determine why he blew up so easily, but before I can finish my thoughts, the phone rings again. Still in his hand, he answers it walking away from me. Autumn is starting to cry but instead of tending to her, I follow him. Curiosity pulling me forward while the pace of my heart is quickening like it's trying to win some invisible race.

"Yo! Don't know who the fuck this is or why you are fucking blowing up this number, but you need to cut the shit out and stop calling here." For the first time I hear the caller speak right before he disconnects the call.

"You know who that is?" I say in a hushed tone more to myself than to him. Autumn is starting to scream, and milk is leaking letting me know it's time to feed her. I go into the bedroom and pick her up out of the crib with Nathan right behind me.

"No, I don't know who that is? Why would you even ask that?"

"Because. Never once did I get a response." Choose your next words carefully, I tell myself. "Not one time during all these calls did they speak." My heart must have finished its race because it has come to a sudden stop.

"Nathan? I believe I heard a woman's voice." I say looking into his eyes for answers that would explain this soap opera cliff hanger. But unlike a soap, I don't have the weekend to wait to see what will happen. Seeing nothing there, I make myself comfortable on the sofa to get Autumn latched and control my nerves, so she doesn't feel my agitation. He sits on the ottoman in front of me and lightly caresses the sides of my legs. It's summer and I have on shorts, so his touch automatically relaxes me.

"LaChelle. I don't know who is calling you or why. Feed your daughter and don't answer your phone anymore unless you know the number. I'm going home to get some clothes. Promise me you won't answer the phone."

"You know I can't."
"Do you know how much I love the smoothness of your legs?" He says with a smile and kisses my daughter on the forehead and then kisses me and I kiss him back. As he stands to leave, I get up to follow him to the door.

"Nathan." He stops and looks at me with those deep brown eyes that have a lightness to them. "Please don't have me caught up in any nonsense." Before he can respond, I pull him in for a deep kiss getting as close to him as I can with Autumn between us. However, he breaks it and pulls away.

"Baby, I need you to know I love you and there is no one else that has my heart like you do. I love your kids as if they were mine and here with you guys is the only place I want or need to be. You know this right?"

"I know." I think that I know. No. I thought I knew. Now I'm not so sure.

"You almost made me forget I picked up something for her." From his shoulder bag, he pulls out a small jewelry box.

"Now before you say what TT said, this box is not for you, so it doesn't count." I laugh at this because I know what he is referring to. TT recently told him that he wasn't allowed to give me any jewelry unless he put a ring on my finger first. And if he did buy

54

anything other than a ring, it should come in a paper bag as not to get my hopes up. He opens it to reveal a child's gold necklace with her name written in cursive.

"Babe. This is so pretty. Go ahead and put it on her." I say as I pull her a little away from me for him to put it on. I watch him with hope that he is not playing with me. In the short time we have been together, this man is everything I could ever want, and I say a silent prayer that this caller is not concerning him.

"Alright baby. I'll be back." And with that, he gives us both a kiss and leaves. The moment the lock clicked in place, the phone rung and my heart sank with the feeling that God had just confirmed the two are indeed connected. With no need for formalities, I get straight to the point.

"Nathan just left to go home. Who am I speaking with?" I ask, holding my breath waiting for a response. Nothing. "Don't be shy now. I heard you start to speak before he hung up on you." I look down at Autumn to make sure she is feeding because I feel as if everything in me has gone still. My heart, blood, breath and even my milk.

"Nathan is my boyfriend and we practically live together so whoever this is, speak your peace." LaChelle, breathe. I tell myself as I wait to see if I get a response. "I'm going to hang...."

"His wife." She states. I hang up and freeze as if Dougie E. Fresh told me to.

56

We Have an Issue

She called back and informed me that the reason he was able to stay with me during the week was because she worked nights and had the weekends off. They had just had their first child in May and that she knew he was getting practice with my baby. I was beyond hurt. I had fallen in love with him and knew it would be difficult to just walk away. It would have been easier if I had known from the beginning he was married. One, I never would have talked to him. Two, if I lost my mind and did want to have an affair with a married man, I surely would not have given him my heart.

Once the call is done, I put on Luther Vandross *Superstar*. When he sings *Don't you remember you told me you loved me baby*, I am thankful that Autumn is asleep in her crib. I don't want my sobbing to wake her. Later that evening, he comes back. He wants to know why I've been crying, and I let him know that I spoke to his wife.

"I wasn't happy. My marriage started coming undone months before I met you. I can't turn back time and meet you under different circumstances. She was pregnant with her baby."
"Our." I say cutting him off.
"What?"
"Our. You should have said 'she was pregnant with our baby'."
"Yes. She had our baby but it's over. You of all people should know you can have a baby with someone you are not romantically involved with." This angers me.

"LaChelle? Are you hearing me."
"What do you mean your marriage was over months ago? Was she not pregnant soon to deliver your first child when you met me? What the fuck is your problem?"
"Come here baby."

"Baby? I thought I was just some hoe you were helping." I say satisfied at the look of surprise as I threw his words back at him. "Yep. She called me back that night and I heard your whole conversation."

"Then why were YOU on the line yelling, saying not to call that number again? You're a sad excuse for a husband and a bitch for doing this when I just had our baby."
"I was walking by the house we did work on, and the man's daughter was in her yard crying. I only stopped because we spent three months working on his house and therefore, I remember the family. She ASKED me to say that! I'm telling you; I'm not sleeping with that hoe!"

"LaChelle."
"Nathan"

He is reaching for me, and I take a step away because the last thing I need right now is his touch.
"Give me my keys back right now." I say through clinched teeth wondering if he can see the steam coming from my nose and ears like in the cartoons.
"No. I'm not giving you anything back because this is where I want to be. With you and the kids."
"You are married and it's not fair to me or her! I don't want this karma. You need to leave."

He takes a step towards me, and I turn and go to peek in on my baby. When I close the door and turn around, he is right there. Fresh tears start rolling down my cheeks as I look into those beautiful eyes. Wondering if I see hurt in them? If it is, from what? Making his wife upset? Making me upset? Getting caught?

"You got caught cheating and you trying to patch things up over here. I am not a side chick."
"No. You're not a side chick. I want you to be my main chick. If I met you years ago, you would be my wife now."
"Why? So, you could cheat on me too?"

I freeze as his fingers start to wipe my tears away. I can't move. The number of emotions running through my head is like a crowded train during rush hour. Anger, hurt, horniness, love, hate, tension, frustration, and despair are all multiplied on different levels, and I can't capture the one I need to stand firm in my wanting him out of my home. In my head, I'm begging him to stop touching me. Yet, I just want to kiss those lips.

"I need you to leave." I mean these words even if there is no firmness to them. I don't move when he starts to kiss my tears. Nor when he turns me around and walks me backwards to the sofa. Confusion settles in. *Oh, dear Heavenly Father, why do I want him? No, girl. You don't want him. He probably just finished fucking his wife.* Those lips are moving ever so slowly on my neck to my breasts and I'm still crying while mentally having dialogue. *Don't have sex with him. You know he most likely just fucked his wife. She won't fuck him right now. No? You know intimacy and orgasms don't always come from intercourse. I don't want to have sex with him, but I want to.*

My desire for him is a seesaw going between wanting him and not wanting him. I allow him to do with my body as he pleases. Removing my panties, he continues kissing my inner thighs before reaching his destination sending me into a pleasure I don't want to have. *He can be down there, but we are not having intercourse.* I hate my body for the multiple orgasms his mouth puts me through. When he comes up and kisses me, I relinquish to those soft full lips that I can't resist. It's slow and intimate and I kiss him for what I believe will be the last time. He enters me and I make love to him holding on for dear life like he is the lifeboat I need in these choppy waters. I don't stop when Autumn starts to stir. This will be the last time we will be like this, and I need to savor every moment.

But it wasn't the last time. After that night and the next, I escaped to Bushwick for a week just to get away from him. Passing my cousin Stacey's house (no blood relation) my eyes fell on this very sexy guy sitting on the stoop smoking a cigarette and drinking coffee. Our eyes locked and a tingle went down my spine. He was fine, sitting there in his baseball cap, white tee and dirty jeans looking muscular and sexy. I nodded a hello and proceeded to my mom's stopping at TT's where she was sitting outside with my aunt and uncle.

As Kamar went to go get his bike (this six-year-old first grand and first great-grand (on TT's side) had three sets of toys and bikes at each place he stayed) I filled them in on what happened with Nathan through all the tears that continued to fall.

After the week was over and on our way home, I stopped at Stacey's to find out if she knew the guy from earlier. Unbeknownst to me, he had already inquired about me and wanted me to go to the garage next door where he was working on a car so he could formally introduce himself.

I went.

Going around the car, I saw him deep under the hood. "Excuse me. I heard you wanted to meet me?" I said with a little hesitation in my voice.
"Ah yes. I wanted to meet the princess of Hancock formally. I'm Chase." He wipes his hands on a rag so we can shake.
"LaChelle."
"Only good things have been said about you LaChelle." He said with a smile on his face showing a row of teeth any dentist would be proud of.
Laughing "I don't know what you heard, but I am no princess."
"Don't sell yourself short. From what I know, your grandmother is like the Queen of the block which makes you the princess."
"Yes. She is very well respected and classy if I do say so myself."
My heart drops when he walks closer to me because I see that he is a few inches shorter than me. I'm 5'7 so he is about 5'5.

Kamar comes in and joins me and they share a proper high-five. He then peeks in the stroller and states "this will work."
"Excuse me? Are you some kind of open pedophile? What the hell you mean by that?" But I don't wait around for an answer. I swing the stroller around so we can leave.
He taps my shoulder, "Hold on. I meant nothing nefarious about it. My son is seven. Pursuing a relationship with you and your kids would work. He lives in Delaware. You can ask about me."
"I might just do that. Have a nice evening." Which comes off sarcastically as I am walking away.

Approaching my apartment, I see Nathan leaning on his car in front of my building.

"Who was that nigga you were talking too?" He asked angrily.
"Don't know what you talking about?
"Nah you know. That little light skinned nigga you were talking to at Stacey's before you came here?"
"So, you're following me now?"
"I went there to see why you weren't here and I saw you talking to him with your bags, so I knew you were coming home. Who is he?
"How's your family?" I ask.

This softens his speech to me, but I ask him to leave and go home. How does asking him to leave end up with us in bed? Absolute weakness and stupidity on my part. When he does leave, he tells me he loves me and that I will be his wife as he is going to get a divorce. I ask for my key back. He just looks at me then leaves. Same scenario the next day. Then silence.

In this silence I am losing my mind. My heart hurts and damn all the love songs I keep replaying. Admonishing myself because he finally left me alone. Gave me what I wanted yet, hating it. I knew this was best as I was not happy with the actions of sleeping with him when I knew for a fact, he had a wife and baby at home. I didn't know what to do with these emotions for I still deeply loved and wanted him, knowing it wasn't right.

It's just that day I met him Downtown Brooklyn, I felt in every fiber of me that I was looking at my husband. I have never felt that way before. And now knowing that he was already someone's husband tore me into pieces. He was good to me. Good to my kids. How could I just turn my emotions off like a faucet?

Then the blackout happened. I was sitting on the stoop with my cousin when he walked up pushing a stroller. I see him in his baby's face.

"Why are you here?"
"Because I wanted you to meet my baby."
"Adorable. But you shouldn't be here."
"This is my child, and we can go wherever I want and see whoever I want. When my divorce is finalized, we will be a family."
"Please leave." But I can't take my eyes off his baby. Nathan's features jumping out at me and trying to get an idea of what the mom looks like.
"I'm going to come back. Do you need anything?"
"No but thank you for asking."
"I don't want you leaving anywhere when it gets darker. Stay inside and I'll be back."
"Please stay with your family tonight. I can take care of mine."

Watching him leave, I felt like I was falling into a deep well. Solidifying my situation of being still madly in love with someone else's husband.

We were still outside hours later as the weather was cooler, and the sky showed off all the stars we normally didn't get to see. My cousins and I were debating if we were seeing the face in the moon when Nathan showed up again asking if he could speak to me inside.

"Nate. Mommy had to climb through the window because the door locked when I got my popsicle. She went up the fire escape and everything." He says in the cutest way that only little kids retell stories.
"Yeah. And what happened?" He asked kneeling to Kamar's level.
"She got Autumn out the crib and came back outside."
"Autumn was still in the house?"
"She was sleeping. Didn't even wake up when mommy knocked a dish over coming through the window."
I asked him how he knew so much.
"Because I wanted to see you break in mommy." He says laughing.
"Alright little man. Good that you were watching your mommy's back." He says handing him a five-dollar bill.

Kamar and Autumn stayed outside with my cousins when we went in. After a short conversation of how I couldn't see him anymore, we end up having sex and he left right afterwards leaving my key on the nightstand. I knew he was done. I knew it was best because I hated me for sleeping with him. I didn't like it and knew I needed a distraction to get him out of my system. The next day with the lights still out, we made our way over to Bushwick. There I saw Chase and invited him over.

Should've Just Read My Bible

Chase came to the house on a Friday evening. We talked for several hours straight getting to know each other. He then left and came back later that night. While Chase and I were chatting, my doorbell rang and when I went to the front door, I saw Nathan on the other side. When I denied his request to enter my home, he wanted to know if I had someone there. Told him no and if I did, it wouldn't be any of his business. As he tried to force his way into my apartment, we got into a pushing match.

He pulled out a knife yelling and threatening to stab whoever was inside. It wasn't until the neighbor from upstairs threatened to call the cops did he leave, while calling me every name but my own. Watching him leave the block and turn the corner, I went back into the house. Chase heard the commotion and decided to leave letting me know he wasn't for the drama. Questioning if I had set him up for a fight. This was far from the truth, but he didn't want to hear it and left.

A few days had passed before I heard from him again. He told Stacey what went down and how I tried to set him up for an altercation. He was advised that I wasn't like that and had just broken up with my boyfriend whom I had found out was married. This must have put him at ease because he later ended up on my doorstep with a dozen roses and an apology. *Guess he didn't realize or care that he did the same thing Nathan did and just showed up unannounced.*

I forgave him for selfish reasons. I needed someone to take my devastation away. That night, we stayed up until the next morning talking and instead of leaving, we went to bed where I really forgot about Nathan. The next evening, he wanted to take me out. I got dressed up then cancelled on him because I didn't own a pair of flats. Still uncomfortable with being taller than him.

Especially in my heels, I suggested we stay in and watch a movie. He informed me that heels were a turn on for him.

The first bar we went to was low key and quiet. We talked over appetizers and a round of drinks. After that, we left for someplace a little livelier and louder. We ended up at a gay bar in the Village where I drank and sung Whitney Houston's *How Will I Know* on karaoke. It was one of the best dates since graduating from the University and the last time we spent a night on the town. As I threw up coming out of the train station, he hailed a cab to take me home. There, he helped me get into my night clothes and tucked me in the bed. Then in the morning, I thanked him for being a gentleman by not taking advantage of the situation.

He ended up moving in a few weeks later. *Yeah, yeah, yeah, I know what you're thinking and you're probably correct. But! If you are thinking of Kamar, let me clarify something. When I say that Nathan practically moved in, it was only because he had a key. He had no clothes or personal belongings other than a toothbrush and deodorant. Most times when he was over, it was after dinnertime, and he was always out of the apartment before it was time to wake Kamar up for school. He was not the type of child to sleep with me. He slept in his own bed in his own room.*

Now when Chase moved in, he didn't have a lot of anything. Just a duffle bag and even with him, it wasn't a next day time of thing for Kamar. Since he still visited with his dad every other weekend, it was a while before I sat him down to explain that Chase was going to be staying here.

And let me also say regarding both Nathan and Chase, I did not leave my kids with them. When I left, they left and if I was just running to the corner store, my kids went with me. They were my babies and my responsibility. Both men played with Kamar around me. I wasn't going to entrust their safety to just anyone. I always prayed to God that no man would come into my life and hurt my babies. It wouldn't be until I was pregnant with Chase's child that I allowed him to walk Kamar to school and pick him and Autumn up from after school/daycare, but I've jumped ahead. Let's get back to my story.

Not sure how it happened or when; it just did. During this time, I came to learn a few things about him. He believed in God but had more faith in the Illuminati and other brotherhoods. He would fall asleep in the middle of a conversation, while eating or smoking. This sudden sleeping was blamed on medication or just exhaustion from working construction all day. *If you're thinking that I should probably stop messing with men in the construction field, I would agree. But a man that works with is hands is a turn-on. An older cousin once told me that a man who knows how to work with his hands will never have a hungry family.* And Chase not only worked in construction, but he also worked on cars as a hobby.

One night he sang me the song *Don't Change* by Musiq Soulchild and told me he loved me. I couldn't say it back. I started feeling that this short-term distraction had gone too far, but I forced myself to start having feelings for him. It wasn't hard to do. Our sex life was becoming more intense and that is what I fell in love with. That was enough for me. Plus, he was good to the kids.

He did thoughtful strange things like change around my whole apartment when I took the kids to visit Asha out of state. When I asked why he did it, he replied, "I was bored." He also did the most romantic and thoughtful things. Like buying the cassette of Eddie Murphy's album because he knew how much I loved the song *How Could It Be* and a *Barnes and Noble* limited addition Scrabble board because it was my favorite board game.

On Thanksgiving Day, he got down on one knee and proposed. I said yes, although my mind was screaming *NOOOOO*. I couldn't see myself hurting his feelings. We set a date for next year and I started planning.

In early December, Nathan called and asked if he could stop by and if I needed anything. It was snowing and Autumn had developed a fever. I asked if he could pick up Children's Tylenol since Chase would be gone for a few hours. When he came, he spoke to the kids and let me know that he still loved me and I truly still loved him. More than I loved Chase. He was still married and visibly hurt when he saw the delicate ring on my finger. We shared a kiss at the door for old times' sake, and I melted in that kiss realizing that I might have made a grave mistake in letting this thing with Chase go on for so long. *But he is still married so part lips and send him on his way.* And that I did. Crying while closing the door on what I knew to be the last time we'd see each other.

By January, Chase and I had put deposits down for the DJ ($125), reception hall ($250), caterers ($250) and my wedding gown ($500). In February, shortly before Autumn's first birthday, I found out I was pregnant. At the beginning of March, with the wedding only a few months away, he sat me down to tell me he couldn't marry me because he was still legally married. *What in the fucking hell? Did I have a radar that told marry men to approach me? I guess a girl does choose men like her father. Mine were liars.*

"What do you mean you are still married?" I asked enraged.
"We have been separated for two years but hasn't signed the divorce papers yet."
"So why in heaven's name would you ask me to marry you, put all this money out and you knew all along that you weren't available for marriage?"
"I'm sorry."
"I'm sorry? Is that all you can say? These past months we have been moving like a family. You go to church with me. What the hell am I supposed to say besides the wedding is off."
"I'm sorry. I let her know she needs to sign them...."

I cut him off asking what the holdup is, but I don't stick around for a reply. I think about the that money down the drain, upset doesn't begin to describe how I felt. Stupid, misled, bamboozled and tricked. Wondering where and what was going wrong in my life that I allowed this to happen. Questioning if it was a prank to get back at me for only being with him at first just to get over Nathan. Nathan, who after that night I never heard from again. I went to the bedroom to think and cry.

After a few days, my anger diminished, and we put our focus on him trying to get a divorce. The hurt and embarrassment were present as I let everyone know the wedding was delayed until an unforeseeable future. Postponed with an indefinite timeframe. The only bright side of not getting married while pregnant was that I would be able to drink and have a good time at my own reception. Whenever and if it ever took place.

As we continued playing house, his personality went through changes. He would be extremely happy for a few days, to withdrawn for days. He'd get excited for business adventures like starting his own moving company or ridiculous schemes like money-chain letters. Then, not have energy and drive to go to work for a length of time.

One day, he went into the bathroom and ate chicken wings. When I asked him why he did it, he swore he didn't. Mind you, there were chicken crumbs around the toilet and the bathroom smelled of chicken from the Chinese place. When he continued to deny it, I commented that living with him was like living with different people except they all liked having sex. Rough and dominating or soft and sensual, I never knew which Chase I would get, but it didn't matter because I enjoyed all of it. It wouldn't be until later that I found out this was a very true observation.

Sometime in September on the way back from picking Kamar up from school. He is pushing Autumn in her stroller when we see Nathan coming out of the train station.

"I see you got on with your life." He says looking at my protruding belly.

"Yes. How is your family?"
"I'm going to be a dad again." Oh! The knife in my heart twists.
"You and your wife?"
"Yes. We worked things out."
"Glad to hear that for you." Feeling another twist of the knife.
"Well. It was nice seeing you. Enjoy your life." *Don't you dare cry.*
"Chelle. I want you to know I will never stop loving you." I tell myself again not to cry.
"And I will always love you. Bye."
He gives Kamar a hug and a kiss for Autumn. For me he has a hug and whispers in my ear "That should be my baby you carrying." And walks away but not before I catch his eyes getting misty.

I watch him until he turns around, locking eyes with me. I turn and go about my way in my own thoughts. Only snapping out of it enough to pick up something for the kids to eat. I try my best to focus on everything Kamar is telling me about school but I'm only half listening because I am saddened at the direction life has taken me and Nathan. In my head I'm thinking, *he lied the day he met you. He doesn't deserve your love or emotions. We are happy with Chase and our growing family.*

As the month went by and Teagan made her arrival, playing house was not enough. Going to church knowing I was fornicating and shacking up became an unbearable weight. I wanted to get married. Leaving him until that happened wasn't an option. The sex was explosive and addictive.

With him, I found that I loved submission and domination. A slap to the face, calling me out my name, choking and all-around roughness was enjoyable, but ONLY in the act of sex because it was with passion. When he did make the mistake of choking me outside of intercourse during an argument, he got kicked out for a few weeks. That choke was not gentle. It had anger and viciousness behind it. Days of apologies worked, and I allowed him back home with the understanding that he had revoked all his rough sex privileges.

Later, as we outgrow my two-bedroom apartment in Crown Heights. We moved to a three-bedroom, one-bathroom apartment in Bed-Stuy. Our location changed but what didn't was my desire to be married. I brought it up constantly. I was serious in that desire that it turned me off from sex. For a few months I couldn't bring myself to be intimate with him. During that time, he started drinking heavily.

He wanted to go out one night but was too drunk to drive. When I tried to take the car keys from him, we started struggling a little. I didn't know he stabbed me with a key until later that day. I couldn't figure out why I was having pain in my stomach. When I found the source of the pain, it was the shape of a key embedded into my skin. I wasn't angry because I knew it was an accident. He was very remorseful and decided to lay off the alcohol for a while. I do want to insert here a drinking story that happened.

I had fixed an apple pie for dessert and put it in the oven. Within a few minutes, the smell of urine became strong. I checked the babies thinking they had an accident on the floor. As the minutes ticked by, the smell became stronger. I went through the apartment trying to find the source of the stench. Finally, I realized that the smell was strongest by the oven. I opened it up and was hit with the worst smell imaginable. *How did I miss it when I put the pie in?* He mistook the oven for the toilet. I went to the bedroom and woke him up from his nap and told him what he had done. The shame on his face as he cleaned the oven was too funny to be angry. I was only upset that I had to throw my pie away. That night we made love like lost lovers who found their way back to each other. We also conceived.

Lessons Not Learned

I was heated with the positive results of the pregnancy test. Here we were about to have another baby out of wedlock. The nagging for marriage resumed. I pressured him to be his wife, and he promised I would be. As I suffered through all-day sickness, he took care of me and the kids. When we were coming out of the supermarket one day, he held my hair out my face and rubbed my back as I vomited between cars. This type of attention caused me to love him again. Sex came back into our lives on daily basis like when we first got together making us both giddy and determined to commit ourselves to each other.

When I was about two months in, I started spotting at work and went to the hospital in fear of having a miscarriage. There, they took a blood test and told me that my hCG levels were high and an ultrasound was needed. "You are not having a miscarriage, but you are having twins." I was elated and scared. Plenty of women in my family have had twins, yet none of them survived. I became classified as a high-risk pregnancy and received their due date of August 14th. I was assured that all multiples were classified this way, and it was no cause for alarm.

Chase wasn't with me at the hospital, so I called him right away. He was excited and told me he'd pick me and the kids up from Stacey's house (which was around the corner from the daycare). While waiting for Chase, I showed the sonogram to TT, my mom and Kamar. His scream of joy was contagious pushing the fears of previous outcomes in my family aside. I fed off Chase and Kamar's excitement as best I could. It was a hard thing to do when family history matters.

By February, I was three months looking as if I was six. Morning sickness lasted all afternoon and into the night. Chase was laid off and actively seeking work to provide for his growing family. He tried his hand at selling real estate and gave up after a few days. I found this strange because he never went to school to get his license but then who was I to question him? *Only his baby mama.*

When he found work at a warehouse, the drinking started again. He became an angry drunk. Quick to start an argument. One evening, he left to pick the kids up from Bushwick at five. Around 8pm, I started calling my family to send him home because I was getting worried and upset. Thankfully, TT had given them dinner so all I had to do was get them into bed. She told me he was very talkative and animated.

When I asked if he was drunk, she said, "Do you think I would let my babies get in the car with him if he was drunk? He did have a beer but that was it. He was all over the place with his conversation even before he had the beer which is why I kept him here longer just to make sure he wasn't on anything else."

I made up my mind that when he came in, I would not say anything. Just put the kids to bed and let him talk, if that was what he wanted to do. Even when he bought them back a whole two hours after leaving Hancock, I was determined not to yell or unleash the fury I was holding inside. He found my silence amusing and went from yelling to laughing then back to yelling. I was confused and wanted no parts of whatever was going on with him.

Once the kids were in bed and I was coming out of the bathroom from getting myself ready for bed, he started pushing me all while having a one-sided argument. I asked him to keep his voice down and his hands off me, I wasn't trying to argue.

This pissed him off and he pushed me into the wall with all his strength. He waited until I got my bearings before pushing me again. This went on until he got tired of my trying to get away without arguing back at him. Kamar came out of the room just as he pushed me again followed by Autumn. I told him to take his sister to his bed and close the door and not come out. Chase then pushed me to the floor, got on top of me and started choking me.

I scratched and clawed trying to get him to release me. I was getting lightheaded, and breathing was getting difficult. I saw Kamar come from the room and panicked. From the corner of my eye, I saw Teagan's Jack-in-the-Box, grabbed it and swung it directly at his head with everything in me. He fell off and when I stood up, Kamar was opening the door for the police to come in. Our next-door neighbor called them, but we didn't hear the knocking.

By the time I called my mom to come over, there were more than six officers in our place. A few were standing around. Some were talking to Chase at the dining room table, and I had some in our bedroom explaining to me why I had to leave the apartment. According to the female officer, Chase had some scratches on his face, and his shirt was torn indicating an altercation.

"I'm sorry. I'm three months pregnant with his twins. Was I supposed to let him kill me? Never mind that my kids are home, right?" I asked with disgust.
"You need to see what we see. He has evidence of a fight whereas you don't."
"I am much darker than him and I'm sure his fingerprints would be glaring on my neck if I was as light as him."
"Whose name is on the lease?"
"Both of ours."
"With both of your names on the lease, we can't force him out just because you want him out."
Flabbergasted I asked. "What do you mean? He had me on the floor choking me after I wouldn't argue with him, but I must go!"
"Do you have somewhere for you and the kids to go?" She asks while writing stuff down on a notepad.
"Yes. This is my mom, and I guess you are giving me no choice but to pack my babies up this late at night and leave."

She steps out to go speak with her superior who had arrived and is talking to Chase. Two officers are in the bedroom with me and the kids while I start getting clothes together, remarking to my mother at how unbelievable this situation is. That, because I fought back to protect myself and our unborn babies, I'm the one being penalized. One of the officers begins to explain that they could take us both to the precinct, but they are trying to think about the kids. I say that they are thinking highly of my kids by making them leave their home at almost midnight on a school night.

The superior comes back to ask me who is TT? I'm confused but answer that she is my grandmother and tell him what she told me earlier about his ramblings. He excuses himself and I interrupt to ask, "If we are being made to leave, could we go now? My kids need to get some sleep." He tells me to wait and goes back to talk with Chase.

I am cursing softly because the kids are on my bed and profanity flows easier in ridiculous moments such as this one. He returns to inform me that they are taking Chase down to the station and advises if I decide to file charges (which he recommends), they will start the paperwork for an order of protection effective immediately. I must ask.

"What the hell did he say for the turnaround?"
"He is talking about your grandmother TT? (looking at me to see if he got the name right) Trucks, the weather, you, and other random things. For a person who said they didn't take anything and only had a beer, he is very incoherent. He goes from talking fast with his hands to not saying much. For your safety, you might want to see about getting him removed from the lease and your locks changed."
Stunned. I ask. "Do I have to go to the station to sign paperwork?"
"No. My officer is on their way back with a restraining order for you to keep on you in case we must let him go."

I don't hear anymore. My mind is too busy wondering what the hell did he say to them so calmly at the table for them to give me an immediate restraining order? Granted, he was at the other end of the apartment so I couldn't hear what he was saying. I found that whatever he was saying to them to give me an immediate restraining order scarier than him choking me.

The officers and Chase left. Shortly around one in the morning my mom went back home. After the kids were sound asleep, I went into the bathroom and smoked one of his cigarettes. The next day, I had another one. That night another but this time I didn't smoke it. Once I got it lit, I went through the motions of smoking it without taking it to my lips letting it burn out. I didn't smoke during my other pregnancies and didn't want to start now. However, these were different and difficult circumstances.

I found taking care of the kids while constantly being sick trying. I was exhausted and had to find the energy after a long day at work, picking them up, going over homework and playing with them. Getting them dinner and off to bed left me zapped. This is why by the middle of March, he was back.

He found a trucking job driving at night and home during the day to sleep while I was at work. Our paths crossed at dinnertime. We were finished. A fractured relationship that didn't need mending. When we spoke, it was only of the kids, the twins and the bills. The month ended with him out of work again and all the cash in his pocket for April's rent gone. When I asked how he lost the money, he replied,

"I was robbed coming out the check cashing place." I genuinely felt bad for him although I was hotter than the night when the lights when out over the city about the lost cash. But, like those nights where we had no choice but to make the best of the situation, I had no choice but to try and come up with the money.

As he began drinking again, we continued the dance of avoidance as if he was still working. The last blow up we had was over the boy's names. He wanted to name them J and K. Not any variation of Jai, Chase, Jae, and Kay, Kai, Kae. He literally wanted to name them letters. I made him mad by laughing because I truly thought he was joking.

"Why give them letters instead of names?" His argument was that I got to name Kamar and Autumn *remember, not his kids*, and he only got to give Teagan her first name. He wanted to teach me that I can't have things my way all the time and they were going to be named J and K. When I stated that those are not names but letters, he argued and argued. When I was done listening, he argued with himself and kept telling me how I can't control everything.

The month of April became proof of that.

Stay Right Where You Are

The morning of April 6, 2006, started as an ordinary day. Got the kids up and dressed for school and daycare, then off to work. Heading to the train station, a contraction stopped me in my tracks. It was strong, but it didn't last long. I had been having little ones since the day before and didn't pay much attention to them. It was too early for contractions, figuring it was just the boys changing positions on me. But then, having given birth to three kids already, I knew what they felt like. Two weeks earlier I had started leaking milk and figured that's what the body did with multiples. As I worked, they got closer.

By the time I left for work around five, I called Chase and my mom to let them know I was heading over to the hospital to be on the safe side. My contractions were now coming in about twenty minutes apart. I was dreading the wait at the hospital, hoping they wouldn't need to keep me. I walked up to the ER desk and let them know that I was twenty-two weeks, with contractions coming twenty minutes apart and my breast had started leaking milk.

I was taken to a bed and hooked up to the machine that produced a steady printout of the contractions at the high, low and resting phases. This printout looks like an EKG or lie detector test, with a line going up, down and straight. Once I was comfortable as one can get with that big wide band that you're not supposed to move with around my belly, the nurse asked me how I was feeling and if I was in any pain.

"No."
"You just had a strong contraction."
"I know but it feels like mild menstrual cramps."

"Your chart says you started leaking milk? It's too early for milk to be produced to the point of flowing unless you are nursing." She states still reading the printout.

We continue chatting about little things as we are both watching the moving points on the printout. As I look at the line about to rise indicating a contraction is about to come, I say a prayer.

As I lay there listening to all the activity in this open area with only curtains between us patients, I fight back tears and call Chase to give him an update. He says "Don't cry. Everything is going to be ok. These boys are going to be healthy and spoiled. Your body is just confused. Everything is going to be ok."

The doctor comes over and reads the printout.

"Well Miss Burroughs, you just had another contraction. Usually with twins early labor comes, but we don't want to see these twins this early. What we are going to do is give you an IV of Terbutaline. This will stop the contractions allowing them to continue growing. Once they stop for a few hours, we will let you go home. Sound good?"
"Will it harm them?" As the tears start welling up in my eyes. *Don't you dare fall!*
"No. It will just stop the contractions. No harm to them."
"Then it sounds good. I would like to sleep in my own bed tonight."

Two hours later, I am given another dosage because the contractions have not stopped. Five hours after first walking into the ER, I am admitted. My mom lets me know the kids are staying with her and she hasn't heard from Chase. *Neither have I since I last called him.*

I wish I could re-count each day with the happenings of those days, but I can't. If you have ever had a stay in the hospital, you know the days start to morph together. I can't even recall if or

80

when my babies came to visit. I had visitors most days like my mom, TT, and cousins and talked with lots of people on the phone. Became familiar with some of the nurses that they would take dinner or lunch with me if no one was visiting. I can't recall each day as it happened, but I would like to tell you about a few significant events that did occur. Events that my mind still goes back to.

Banning Chase

After I was admitted to the hospital, I left a message for Chase about my room number, status, and who the kids were staying with. He called me back to let me know he was coming and wanted to know if I could eat and if so, what did I want. The boys liked spicy foods and fish sandwiches with hot sauce were their favorite. That is what I asked for. I nibbled over the not-so-bad hospital food because I had a fish sandwich coming my way. We could taste the hot sauce on the two pieces of whiting fish between white bread. If you are a New Yorker, you know the delicious simplicity of a fish sandwich with a side of seasoned crinkled fries.

When he showed up, he showed up empty handed. I will admit this made me upset. The boys and I had started salivating for that fish sandwich. I was disappointed for three. After asking and hearing he just didn't feel like stopping, I looked at him and wondered, *at what point did he stop becoming the man that I loved? Did I even still love him like that?* All the same questions that rolled through my head these last few months, along with learning how to dance around him to not set off.

Chase picked up my chart and flipped through it reaffirming what the doctor and nurses have already told me. If they can't get the contractions to stop, they will have to start me on steroids. This was to aid in their development in case of early delivery. I had started nibbling on the snacks the hospital hands out while

Chase was reading the printout asking me if I was feeling the contractions.

"No." I told him.
"They look like they are coming at fifteen minutes apart. And you are not feeling them?"
Again, I told him, "No. My sac is intact, and I haven't dilated which are all good signs. I'm in quiet labor."

At some point, the subject of money and the kids came up. He had started working again and I was struggling trying to carry all the bills myself. I will not put the blame on him by saying he brought it up, nor will I put the blame on myself because I don't remember. It could have been either one of us. Chase started working, he could have needed more money to get to and from work and for lunch. I could have asked, knowing he had started working, to give my mom a little of what we had in the house to help with the kids if he didn't need it. No matter who started, money was the subject of the argument. Then it went back to the fight in February.

Something I found out about Chase early on was to never argue with him. Everything is fair game, even if it happened months or years ago. ESPECIALLY, if he is in one of his "different" stages. Mellow, playful, hustling, in a good mood, even a little agitated, he won't argue. He will have disagreements with statistics and enlightening conversations. For hours. Literally, hours. Angry, drunk or highly agitated, don't argue with him. He won't stop, and he will bring up things that have nothing to do with the subject at hand. I learned that you could never win a case when he was like this and the only option to calm and distract was through sex. This was a little difficult for me, but I tried and failed. I was being a little selfish in this attempt, although feelings for him were up in the air, I knew if I pleased him, that fish sandwich would be on my hospital tray in no time. And dammit, we wanted that sandwich.

Unfortunately, there would be no sandwich because there would be no calming him down. We were both angry and as the profanity started flying, I took on the role I had learned so well. Just to be quiet. Act like I'm listening while my mind goes off in a rant that cannot be spoken. I pick up his words when he goes in on the fact that the kids are not staying with him. Now I've been tagged into back in the ring.

"Chase, I don't want to be worried about the kids right now. They are fine with my mom. Could you please take some money to her?"
"Fuck your kids."

Now I know he didn't mean these words and said them out of anger. In my emotional state, those words cut. They stung with the same amount of venom they were said with. I turned my head and asked him to leave, not wanting him to see the tears forming. Here I am. On a hospital bed. With his twins inside me. Medicated so our sons will have a chance, and he tells that? He is yelling that I better not let anything happen to his sons. I started begging him to go in between sobs. Raising my voice at him asking him to just leave me alone.

After a few minutes of arguing, security comes in and asks him to leave. He says he is going as he stands to walk out of the room. "You better take care of my boys!" This is the last thing I hear him say as he walks out the door. The doctor and nurse walk into the room after Chase and security leaves. I want to note that security did not have to put any hands on him. He walked out of the room on his own. The nurse starts to take my vitals as the doctor hands me a box of tissues and stands at the foot of my bed. She announces that my blood pressure is up, and my pulse is elevated. *Duh! I did just have a fight with the father of three of my babies, of course I'm upset.*

"You can't afford to be upset. Your pregnancy is very high risk. Your contractions haven't stopped. I do not want to have to

deliver these babies now because their chances of survival will be tough. No one else matters but you. You and your sons are my patients and as my patients, I need to tell you what needs to happen. You need to stay relaxed and calm while you are here. We do not want anything to bring this delivery on. High blood pressure can cause your body and your babies harm that we don't want. Are you listening to me?"
"Yes Doctor. I hear and understand you."
"The health of these babies are the only things that matter. I am sending a social worker in here to let you know your options." Spoken with sincerity.

The tears continued their path down my face. The nurse rubbed my arm, wiped my tears and told me to calm down. She wanted to go home on time and if these babies came, she would have to stay. That got a laugh out of me just as the social worker came in. The nurse left, and the social worker took a seat next to my bed. She informed me that the doctor told her of a verbal argument that went on for several minutes in this room.

"He was notified by the nurses at the station who called security. He also said that at the risk of your babies, you absolutely cannot get stressed out."
"Being in the hospital is stressing me out."

She agreed but said that I was at the only place to get the care these babies needed right now.

"There is a temporary ban I can have him placed on that would ban him from the hospital until delivery. This would mean he could not come into your room or be allowed into the hospital. When he requests a pass, a maternity ban would be shown by his name. The ban would be lifted for delivery, and he would have access to the nursery. Do you want to place him on it?"
"If for some reason, I went into labor, would he be allowed in the delivery room?"

"Yes. He would also be able to go to the nursery. This is only a precaution to make sure you don't go into labor at the cause of any undue stress."
"Do I have to answer you right now?"
With a small sigh, she informs me that she will leave the paperwork, and she strongly advises that I sign it.

I was still upset. I called my sister and tried to tell her everything through fresh tears. She told me she wouldn't listen if I didn't stop crying. "Are you supposed to be crying and getting upset? Aren't you in the hospital because they can't stop your contractions? If the recommendation is to ban him, he is grown. He will build a bridge over his hurt feelings and walk across it."

God. I don't know what to do. And why am I acting like I don't know this man's temper. Lord. Give me the strength to deal with the repercussions. I then signed the paperwork.

PS: TT ended up bringing my fish sandwich.

<u>Weight Gain</u>

My body had taken on a drastic change due to all the medications and steroids. The extended combined use had caused my vagina to swell and extend out to the middle of my thighs. You read correctly. My vagina grew to the size of a basketball right between my thighs. My legs grew twice their size. I had to sit on a pillow of ice to help the swelling go down. When my cousin Samantha came to visit, I had just gotten back in bed from icing myself on the rocking chair. With a flourish of throwing back the sheet, I asked her, "If I wasn't your cousin, would you eat this out?" She jumped back with a start.

"Hell no! Cover that monstrosity up!" She says cringing and taking some of the sheet to put it back over me but acting like she scared to get close.
"Why not?"

"It's not natural." Rubbing her arms and moving like she got the heebie jeebies.

"Go ahead and poke it. See if it'll move like jelly." I say trying my best to keep a straight face but failing.

"Hell no! That shit looks like it's about to fucking burst!"

"So, is that a no?"

"No! That's a HELL NO!"

Oh, my goodness did we have ourselves a good laugh.

This is the first time I regretted not having someone bring me a camera

Easter Sunday

As I was sitting on my pillow of ice on the rocking chair, I felt liquid running down my leg. I pressed the button for the nurse as I made my way back to bed.

I bent my legs at the knees and reached past the swelling to feel where the liquid was coming from. I wasn't thinking anything except that it must be the fluid coming out of the holes I poked. My fear was that my vagina and entire pelvic area would not go back to its original size. *Don't judge. I was trying to help the fluid escape.*

When a nurse that I had not met before came in, he took a small stick and placed it on the fluid. When I asked him what it was for, he said it would tell him if it was amniotic fluid or not. He walked out of the room without telling me the results. One of the nurses I became familiar with came in and asked me how I was feeling as she read the printout. Told her I was fine, and she told me my contractions were coming in less than five minutes apart. Beyond random mild cramping, I wasn't feeling them. As she was re-adjusting the monitor, a doctor that I have not met before came in and said she was going to do an examination to see if I dilated.

"You are NOT sticking your fingers into me. Do you not see how swollen I am?"

"Yes, I do and yes, I am. I must see if you have dilated." *Guess the results were positive for amniotic fluid.*

The nurse that I've come to know says that she will stay with me and that the exam must take place. "It's essential to know if these babies are trying to come now" she states while rubbing my hand. I find comfort in her eyes and that is where I look. That is until I feel the cold gel on my stomach for a sonogram. While the doctor is getting her gloves on, I get a look at my babies known to them as twin A and twin B. To us, we called them by their names assigned to them by my mom. Twin A (on top) is Khalil. Twin B (on the bottom) is Jaden.

Turning my head towards the doctor as she explains that she only wants to see if I dilated. I take a deep breath and exhale ever so slowly. This is repeated two more times as instructed. She thinks I'm calm enough for the exam. Maybe I would have been if every inch wasn't abnormally protruding. She barely gets her fingers in when pain creeps up my spine.

As she goes further, the intensity of the pain feels like I'm being sliced open with multiple razors immediately followed by salt and lemon juice. You know the paper cut you didn't know you had until something gets in it causing it to sting? Magnify that sensation times a million.

"I fucking told you you can't examine me!" I scream.

The nurse by the monitor is trying to get me to look at her while she holds my hand and pushes the hair off my forehead. Due to all the swelling, she isn't getting a good measure of dilation. She rams her hand in again but with a piece of equipment. I am flat on my back, crying feeling like a torture victim. I can't find my breath to curse her out because breathing has become difficult. Vomit is clawing in my throat, and I can't sit up on my own. The nurse next to me had left leaving no one sit me up. Choking on the vomit that is stuck in my throat, my head starts to feel as if it is about to explode, and the room starts to dim. Things are going blurry, and sound is becoming muffled. I start to lose consciousness just as I feel someone grab my shoulder.

With heavy eyelids starting to open, I see a hand holding a bottle under my nose and a stick in my throat causing me to gag and throw up into the waiting bin. The nurse is back but sitting behind me holding me up as the bedrail has been put down. The doctor is gone.

As my breathing regulates, the nurse gives me a squeeze causing me to lay back on her and cry. I don't know if I cried myself to sleep or if they gave me medication to sleep. All I know is while I was crying, the nurses were cleaning my face and when I woke up, TT was in the room. She stopped by to bring me a plate of food. She gave me collards, macaroni and cheese, ham, yams, and a piece of her famous cornbread (seriously. People traveled just for some of her cornbread and greens). You know, the Easter Sunday meal that only grandmothers can pull off? It's just too bad I wasn't hungry. When I looked at her, she demanded to know why there are broken blood vessels in both my eyes. I tried to tell her about the examination, but my throat hurt and I could hardly speak.

When I woke up again, my mother was there sitting in the chair watching T.V. With a scratchy voice, I asked her how long she had been there and about the kids. She told me she was going to bring them, but TT called her and told her not to. That I looked bad due to the blood in my eyes, and she didn't want them to be frightened. She nibbled on the plate of food left by TT and said the kids were over TT's eating. I asked for a mirror and started tearing up again. Through pain, I told her how I almost died from an examination that I felt should not have taken place. Not caring if she was just doing her job.

Monday

The doctor that got the social worker came in to see how I was doing. I complained about my inconsiderate treatment provided to me by his co-worker on call yesterday. He told me that she noted I was two centimeters dilated. He said he would have to examine me and promised to be as gentle as possible. My entire body went tense at those words. Then he said the most wonderful thing. That he was going to numb the area so I wouldn't experience any discomfort. I could have hugged him. While he gloved up and a nurse was doing the sonogram, he asked me about the pain.

"On a scale of childbirth, how bad was the exam?"
"Being that I had natural birth with all my kids, the pain yesterday surpassed them all."
"Tell me about their births."

I did. Told him about all three. Told him that the first time each of them were in my arms I sung the chorus of *Thank You Lord* by Walter Hawkins. How I changed the word done for the word given. *Thank You Lord for all You've given me.*

While the examination was going on, I was transported back in time. I didn't come to the present until he started speaking again.

"I am concerned. I'm going to increase the steroids just in case they come. As of today, you are twenty-four weeks, but I'd like them to have more time. They are sitting on top of each other right now, but they will keep moving around. You haven't dilated past two centimeters, but your contractions are strong and close."

With the exam over, I thanked him for taking my mind off the pressure. Suggested he teach that to his co-worker. Then before the last nurse left, they sat me back on the rocking chair of the ice.

Untitled

Later that evening, my mom had come by to see how I was doing and to bring me something to eat. About thirty minutes after she left, I had the urge to have a bowel movement. I debated about pressing the button for the nurses' station but decided against it. They would always take me to the bathroom, this time, I wanted to do it on my own. I stood up to see if I could balance myself to walk a distance. It was an arduous trek to the bathroom with the monitor on, so I removed it knowing I only had a short window to do this. I looked at my door which was open and used that as motivation to kick start this adventure.

The most I've walked by myself was from the chair to the bed and even when I did that, I got fussed at so getting caught was NOT an option. Walking felt like I was trying to lift fifty-pound weights with each step. I even made boom sounds in my head for each step and almost gave myself away giggling at what I must look like.

Female has bad bed hair that is going in all directions. Blood shot eyes, skinny arms sticking out of a hospital gown holding on to air and the wall for balance. She is walking from side to side unable to walk naturally due to two large legs and holding a? What is that Trevor? I think it's a beach ball between them George. I don't know. At this rate she will make it to the bathroom leaving a trail of raisins. And then the announcers in my head laugh.

Slowly, I made my way to the bathroom squeezing my buttocks to hold the pressure in until I could sit down. I peeked out to see if I saw any nurses standing by. I closed the room door to a crack, leaving the bathroom door open. When I sat down, nothing expelled from my body. Trying not to strain, I mentally willed the waste to depart from me. After a short moment and nothing happened, it dawned on me that the anal pressure I was feeling could be labor. Reaching between my legs, I felt the smoothness of hair. Fear took over and I became paralyzed, screaming for the nurses with the sense of urgency that matched my increased heart rate. Scared that my babies would fall in the toilet.

Just as I knew, the nurse rushed in and when she saw that I was sitting on the toilet, she reprimanded me. She didn't want to hear the reason why. She called for assistance to get the rocking chair and placed me back on it. The other two nurses that came also gave me a tongue lashing. *If it takes a village to raise a child, then it takes several nurses to fuss at a grown woman for her to feel ashamed.*

As they were pushing the rocking chair back to the other side of the room, I told them that I thought I felt hair. Once they got the chair in front of the T.V. but closer to the bed, one nurse went to get the doctor while one read over my chart, and the other was resetting the machine to put the monitor back on me. They were busy telling me how I was not to get up and move on my on that they forgot to turn me towards the television. They placed me looking towards the door instead. Punishment, I guess.

As they were still in the room, I felt a gush of liquid and looked down. There, facing me was twin B from the bottom, Jaden. I screamed a shrill, "He's here!" while never taking my eyes off him. His face and hand were out on the cold pillow of ice. He waved as if saying *Hi Mommy*.

The first nurse to reach me immediately grabbed him before the rest of him came out and fell to the floor. She started screaming "I need a Code Blue. Code Blue!" and with ease, pulled his neck and the rest of his body out of me. The other nurse that helped me into the chair was gloving on while also calling this code out the door.

Then I heard it over the loudspeaker.

Code Blue.

The universal code for hospitals when a patient is experiencing a life-threatening emergency.

I was this code.

This code, over the loudspeaker, in the hospital was for us. We were in a life-threating emergency.

We were the Code Blue.

Khalil

In the blink of an eye, my room was filled with every nurse on the floor including the doctor from earlier. Someone looked between my legs and was satisfied that the other baby was not peeking out. As incubators were being rolled in and Jaden being taken care of, I was still on the rocking chair stunned. Frozen in time and place. Seeing the activity but not hearing anything beyond the words 'code blue.'

I snapped out of it after the nurse practically hit me hard to ask her question again.

"I need to know if you have any diseases since I handled him without gloves?" I answered no and thanked her for not waiting. And yes, she might have already seen my chart and knew my blood was clean, but that does not take away the disregard of her own health to prevent my baby from hitting the floor.

The doctor started directing them to place me on the bed to prepare the delivery of the second twin. He started explaining that he would have to go in and retrieve him. I asked if he could perform a C-section and he answered that it wasn't possible. I had eaten, and the food mixed with the meds would cause complications. "Could you just leave him alone and let him continue to grow and come out on his own?" The question was not a joke. I really wanted Khalil to stay in if he could. As our dialogue is going on, there is a lot of activity and whispers behind him surrounding Jaden. I am on the bed now and ask to be passed the phone to call my mom.

"Mommy, Jaden is here and I'm about to deliver Khalil. Could you please come back?"

No excitement in my voice. No urgency. No panic. No emotions. Just numbness.

They bring Jaden over to see me before rushing him out of the room to intensive care. He is a beautiful caramel brown with a head full of jet-black hair. "Hi Baby. I love you." I managed to say before they rolled him away. The doctor explains that I will feel a lot of pressure and pain. The enlargement is going to increase this pain and that I needed to make a deliberate effort not to tense up. "Ready or not I have to do this now. We cannot wait any longer." Urgency evident in his tone even though he says it calmly.

I take a deep breath and slowly exhale when the first pain shots up my body and the word fuck escape my lips. Khalil's birth came with pain that my body has never known with any of his siblings. It was so bad that with every pain, I screamed and cursed and for every curse, I apologized. By the time he told me not to tense up for the umpteenth time, I cursed him out, then said sorry. With tears streaming down my face, he then had the audacity to tell me he was ready to go in.

The searing, burning pain is back. Not being tense was an unreasonable request. With every movement of his hands, it felt like I was being ripped apart from the inside out. I don't know if they gave me local anesthesia but if they did it wasn't working because I-FELT-EVERYTHING! And I do mean everything.

It felt like sharp knives carving in each vein from my thighs to my brain while simultaneously ripping a fingernail off on all fingers and toes at the same time. Honestly, I can't explain the intensity of it because I've never felt pain like that before. My body was being traumatized. I was squeezing on the bedrails so hard that one of them fell off. Nurses were on both sides of me to help me push. *They also didn't want a repeat of my near-death experience. No lawsuit for them.* Some of the nurses were getting everything ready for Khalil while some were standing around gloved up and ready to save a life.

After a forever, and several assisted pushes, he arrived. They cleaned him up and I heard the sound of a faint cry. I think, *did Jaden cry? Did I hear him? Oh God please tell me my baby cried.*

When they bought the incubator next to me, I studied him. While they were trying to stick a breathing tube in his nose, I asked, "why is his ear the shape of a spiral?" and commented that he was the same color grey as Kamar when he was born. I looked at him and said, "I love you my sweet baby boy. Jaden is here, and he is just as beautiful as you are."

I asked the nurse if she saw the smile that he just gave. She did and rolled him away to join his brother in intensive care. Before I could say another word, pain redirected my attention. I was asked to push to help expel the placenta although my insides were on fire. The nurses had to continue guiding my body up to push because energy no longer existed for me.

By the time my mom arrived, I was in the middle of cursing through the pain and apology cycle. She told me to watch my mouth, but the doctor came to my defense by telling her how good I was doing and that he wasn't taking anything personally. For the shape my body was in, it was reassuring that I was feeling the pain, and it would be more of a problem if I wasn't.

"She delivered the twins with an enlarged, highly sensitive area and useless medication. I can take a few curse words. Plus, she said sorry after every one of them." He said smiling as he turned to examine the placenta. My back up body (nurses) hugged me and said they were going to check on my boys for me. The doctor then approached bringing with him the placenta to show me where it tore and the discoloration of it. It also had deep holes that looked like craters. He patted my leg and told me he would be right back while the nurses cleaned me up and made me comfortable.

My body, still tense from the trauma, was no longer my focus. Attempting to comprehend and relay the events back to my mom and myself because it didn't seem real. *I was just pregnant an hour ago. What happened?*

Something about my mom I should tell you. She is very unemotional. She doesn't cry. Empathy is not on her face or in her eyes. Sympathy knows no space within her. She can get angry, frustrated and laugh. But in times of heartache, or sadness, she is a blank canvas. A statue. Which can come off as cold when you are spiraling. As I was speaking to her, a doctor from the Neonatal Intensive Care Unit (NICU pronounced nik-u) came in.

"Miss Burroughs. I'm here to talk about Twin B."
"Khalil."
"Yes Khalil. (looking at my mom) Is this your mother?"
"Yes."
"Do you want her to stay?" She asked.
"Yes." I whispered as fear started to tighten in my chest. "What about Khalil? Is it about his ear that's a spiral? Is there something….."

I can't finish as this doctor's eyes have turned red and are getting watery. Time and breathing stopped as tears started streaming down both our faces. *Is it professional of her to be crying?* I wondered but felt comforted by her emotions since my mom wasn't showing any.

There's a mad woman running around in a circle surrounded by flames in my head screaming "lady don't cry. Crying is bad news. Oh God she is going to give us bad news." She drags out the word no, as the flames reach the hanging hair from my scalp. The woman in my head is still screaming as the doctor proceeds to tell us that Khalil didn't make it. My baby has died. The woman in my head collapses as the flames abruptly stop.

I will not make something up just to put here. I know of nothing else after that statement, for I was feeling the literal and not metaphorical breaking of my heart.

Little Faith

Hours later, I was in the NICU awaiting the body of Khalil. While waiting, they rolled me in the wheelchair over to the incubator where Jaden was. In a daze, I studied the infant that is my son. He had a cap on his head, breathing tube in his nose, mask covering his eyes, bandage around his hand holding in the IV, heart monitor on his chest, and a tube going into his stomach. The doctor is explaining everything I see and what they are for.

Most of what he is saying are words flowing in one ear and out the other. He sounds like the teacher from *Charlie Brown*. A few words like blood transfusion, blood on the brain, oxygen, and severe jaundice would slap me across my face. I tried to focus on the statements that contain these words but finding myself unable to. The nurse rolled in another incubator with a gift inside. I stop breathing as the nurse moves me in front of the incubator. Or should I say coffin, because there, wrapped beautifully is my dead baby. *But he can't be.* Another request for a camera has gone unfulfilled.

I stood up and moved my hand around the edge of the package noting how small it is. Marveling at the care of his wrapping. Attempting to prolong the inevitable. My mind returns to a moment in my youth when I was eleven years old. I stayed with Lawrence's youngest sister for a summer in the South.

One night, my dreams were broken by screams coming from her room. I ran to her bedroom pausing at the trail of blood from the bed to the bathroom. She yells for me to take the phone. EMS is on the other end telling me to get her in bed and prop her legs up. Later that evening as I held Alexandria and gave her a kiss, I whispered that her big cousin will always remember her.

As I look at this package, I wonder if Khalil will feel as cold as she did. My heart hurts from all the pieces its broken into. *Breathe. Even in nightmares you must breathe.*

I undid the bow with the tag that had his name and vitals on it. The twine opens and separates. A string up. A string down. Twine going from side to side. Gently I undo the first layer of white chiffon, then the next, until a white blanket is revealed. *Breathe.* Opening the blanket, I see my baby boy. He is perfect. Peaceful. And a little cold. *But this isn't real.* I stroke his head that is full of jet-black hair straight as a fresh perm with strands on the side that had curled up. His nose is slightly angled to the right. His eyes and lips are closed. I count ten fingers and ten toes. One ear is small, but it's the ear that has the shape of a spiral that I trace with my finger. I do this several times wanting to burn it into my memory. I want to take off his pamper so I can see all of him. *They will think that is weird and strange so don't do it.* I don't even though I really want to see all of him. I place my hand on his chest. *Please start beating. Oh God please blow life back into him.* I wait. Nothing. I ask again. And still nothing.

I pick him up to kiss him and hold him close. "Do you know how much I love you my beautiful handsome baby boy. Look at all this hair on your head." I'm rocking him and caressing the side of his face. Telling him how much I love him then it hits me. He's not moving. Not crying. Not breathing. *OH My God he's dead!* I realize that this is the first time I am holding him. After death has already claimed him.
It must have been too much for my mind to process because I see my old friend darkness. This darkness protects me. Nothing exists here. No hurt. No pain. No deceased infant. No baby fighting to live. *Or is he aching to join his identical twin?*

When I woke up and saw my large stomach and the IV hooked into my hand. My first thought was that it was all a dream. A horrible nightmare brought on from stress. As I rub my belly, I notice that the firmness of my boys is no longer there. Neither is the belt from the monitor, and the swelling went down.

As I look around, the room is different. It is smaller and no longer private. There is another bed to the right of me which is currently empty. It wasn't a dream. It is reality. Khalil is dead, and Jaden is not around. The milk streaming from my breasts soils my nightgown. Darkness finds me again.

Nurses, doctors and a social worker make frequent visits pulling me back into this warped reality. Taking vitals, telling me about Jaden, the next steps, hearing and seeing none of them. TT is visiting and wiping away my tears. I laid my head on her chest and felt the change purse as she pulled me closer to her. Then there is commotion outside of my door. When she returns from closing the door, she tells me about Jaden while simultaneously trying to get me to eat.

My mom come in and informs us about the commotion that just happened. Chase came back to the hospital after seeing Jaden wanting to see me. They were on their way to the room to find out if I would see him when he became angry wanting to know what I did or didn't do to cause this. It was then the social work decided that seeing me right now wouldn't be best and had security take him back out.

This is all too much. When TT leaves, my mom takes me to NICU. While we are visiting, he crashes. Like a scene from TV, we were told to move back while they placed little pads on him to jump start his heart. *I think they need to jump mine too.* When they are successful, we are allowed back at his side. The knowledge that Jaden just died lifts the veil of darkness I kept hiding behind. Back at his side, I knew I would have to face this detour. No hiding. No running away. *Dear God, I need a cigarette!*

My mom then told me to have faith in God the size of a mustard seed. For the Bible states that faith that size can move mountains.

But my pain is bigger than any mountain. Deeper than any valley. I would then direct her attention to him. She commented that I didn't have enough faith. That I was focusing on the now, and not what God could do. I told her that I knew what God could do, but He didn't. She shook her head in disappointment and said that she would have faith for both of us. *Oh my God now is not the time. Please leave.* But I didn't say it.

As I looked at my baby with all the tubes and monitors covering his body. Tears fall as I ask the doctor to tell me again what he is suffering through. I want to desperately understand so I can take on his pain. I wanted to hug my baby. Smell him and kiss him while life was pulsating through his veins. When I asked if I could hold him, no was the answer. That he was too fragile. Having to move him from the incubator to me could be enough to send his body into shock. He wouldn't be able to handle it. *I can't handle this.*

Side note: Every time I hear how skin to skin contact is good for preemies to help in their development, I get jealous and question why Jaden and I were denied that. If we had that contact, would I have him to watch grow up?

Back in the room, the social worker came in needing to discuss where I wanted Khalil's body to go. If I would have him buried, cremated or if I wanted the hospital to handle the disposal of his body. The hospital's way sounded like a discard of his existence. I decided to take care of everything. I busied myself by researching funeral homes and cremation prices when I wasn't with Jaden. I did not want my son away from me by being in the ground.

By the time I was released, arrangements were made with the funeral home near my church for cremation. His memorial service was scheduled for after service on the first Sunday of May.

The Reality of Life

Back home, I was on auto as a parent. I got Kamar off to school and the girls off to daycare. Afterwards, I would spend my days at the hospital. Standing next to Jaden, only caressing him in the open areas of his limbs not blocked from tubes. Softly, slowly and gently always mindful of his frailty. I would talk to him about his big brother and sisters. Whenever I would ask if Khalil was with him, he would always smile. This brought me comfort and sadness because I knew he was not alone. His twin was near, but invisible to me.

I would try to hold back tears while speaking to him. I wanted him to feel strength and love, not helplessness and sorrow. I wondered if he felt any pain. Whispering that mommy wishes to take all his discomfort away. Sometimes the tears would disobey and stream down my face anyway. My arms would feel empty and start to ache because they needed to hold him.

My routine after leaving Jaden would consist of picking up Kamar and the girls. Provide a report about their brother. Call NICU. Get them a snack and go over his homework. Call NICU. Playtime then dinner. Call NICU. Once they were in bed, I would once again call NICU. The doctor told me that with Jaden, it was an hour-by-hour situation. They needed to get through an hour. If they could keep him alive for one hour, then they could focus on the next.

At night, fear took over. It kept me awake. Scared that if I slept, I could miss a phone call about him. Chase was not coming around leaving me as the only one to take up post with the phone. The times I would take a nap was in the presence of another adult that could wake me if my phone rang. However, even then, I was aware of surrounding sounds.

I tried watching television, but noise was intrusive to my thoughts. Then I tried watching it on mute, but that still wasn't distracting. I tried the radio; however, I found the music invasive. It was like I wanted to be distracted but I also wanted silence. Nights were the only quite times I had to tell God of my displeasure with Him and yet I wanted something else to think of. *Confusing ain't it?*

To question Him about what I did to deserve this? Why did Khalil have to die? Why is Jaden in so much pain yet unable to cry out? Fear of not being in the hospital with Jaden asking God to be with him all the while telling Him how much this all hurts. Questioning Him on why He needed to take my baby?

Wanting to know if He was going to also take Jaden? If He was planning on taking Jaden, was He going to stop there? Would He also take Kamar, Autumn and Teagan? Needing to know if He was even paying attention to me? Did He not think I could raise my boys? Was this punishment for not trusting Him? Was a family curse at play? Asking Him why He was putting our family through this? Thanking Him for blessing Jaden with another hour. Another day of life. Thanking God for the health of Kamar, Autumn and Teagan, while telling Him how I hated Him for taking Khalil. All these conflicting thoughts were on full display at night.

My mom and sister tried to tell me to think of Job. To read his chapter in the bible of how he lost everything. His children, his livestock, and how he also questioned God and cursed the day he was born. I already knew the story of Job and how he lost everything just to be restored double at the end. I tried to take their advice and read it again for myself. I couldn't get past the first verse.

Job 1:1 There was a man in the land of Uz, whose name was Job; and that man was blameless and upright, and one who feared God and shunned evil. Reading just this verse alone sent me bursting into tears feeling once again that this was all my fault. I caused this because I was not blameless nor upright. I was a fornicator who had five babies by three different men and an abortion. I was nothing like Job and God was punishing me for it.

I, LaChelle Burroughs, was NOT blameless nor upright. I had a fear of God and consequences but held the desires of my flesh higher. And if Job lost everything and endured an attack on his health when he was blameless and upright, where did that leave me?

Please Be Quiet

During this span of time, I started hearing from Chase a little more. When we spoke, it usually turned into an argument over ashes, copies of certificates, or just anything related to Khalil. While reading through sympathy cards, my phone rang with a number I didn't recognize. Naturally my world paused thinking it was NICU calling. The voice on the other end introduced herself as Chase's psychiatrist. She was calling with his permission and on his behalf. My defenses went all the way up. After the greetings and my short responses, she got right to why she was calling.

"It would be beneficial for Chase's therapy if you would come to a session or two."
"For what?"
"To discuss some of the hostility and tension in your relationship."
"Why is he seeing you?" My question went unanswered.
"Why is he seeing you?" I asked with no patience in my voice.
"Chase is Bipolar. The death of his son brought on a mental breakdown."
"And you think it would be helpful for him if I came to a session or two?"
"Yes. It will help you also. We can discover together the cause of your anger."
"Bitch I'm not angry. I'm pissed. Chase is seeing you leaving me to carry this alone! Fuck you, fuck him and fuck your therapy. He is not the only one grieving!"

I hung up the phone with tears running down my face and hatred in my heart. At that moment, I wanted him dead. I prayed for his death. I hated his doctor also. Felt she made him feel like it was okay that he couldn't stand in the fire. Like it was okay that he couldn't be home to take care of the kids and mourn as a family. I wanted them both to go to hell. Thankfully the kids were not home so I was able to have a cigarette.

My soul was tormented. Lack of sleep mixed with all the many emotions and not eating properly was slowly sending me over the edge. There was a slump in my shoulders from the weight of everything I was carrying.

One day I went to buy a pack of cigarettes. Although I was no longer pregnant, I still looked like I was about six months. This guy in a car yelled at me as I lit up that smoking while pregnant was dangerous to my baby. I looked at him and shouted that my baby was already dead.

The cigarettes didn't help though. Neither did drinking. Scriptures, television, nor the radio were helping. Neither were people. No one knew what to say. Whenever anyone stated the below, the retort would either stay in my head or escape from my mouth.

It's all a part of God's plan. *Not my plan. My plan would be pregnant until August.*

God doesn't put more on you than you can bear. *Are you saying that God didn't think I could take care and love Khalil?*

Mourning doesn't last always. *How can you tell me mourning doesn't last always when a piece of me is gone forever always?*

At least you have other kids. *And how does that make anything better?*

What I never fail to understand is why people feel the need to speak? Why can't they let their presence be enough? To care for someone and to love someone are both action words. We show love in how we treat one another. *Abuse of any kind is not love.* The same is true for caring. Be present and if you don't know what to say, say nothing.

In the second chapter of Job when his friends went to see him and saw his sorrow, scripture says in verse 13: *So they sat down with him on the ground seven days and seven nights, and no one spoke a word to him, for they saw that his grief was very great.*

I have heard plenty of sermons about how his friends talked to him when they finally did start talking, but not enough emphasis on the importance of sitting down and shutting up.

When my mom would constantly tell me to have faith that Jaden would make it, I didn't see how he could. A hole in his heart had been discovered. The left side of his brain had started bleeding trying to catch up to the right side that was already housing 1/3 of blood. A shunt would have to be put into his head. He did breathe on his own for 1 ½ minutes before needing his oxygen again so there was a glimmer of progress. But he still needed daily blood transfusions.

The reality of the health of my son did not strengthen my faith. But now my lack of it was weighing on my mind as the reason he was not getting any better. I needed help. Did I already say my soul was tormented?

<u>Gospel Music</u>

One night, sitting on the still new sectional, purchased for our expanding family, crying and thinking, praying for NICU not to call, I remembered a CD that was somewhere in my room. It was the Richard Smallwood Persuaded CD that I'd bought for the song *Calvary*. Once I found it, I put it on and skipped to #7 *Psalm 8*. While the words came pouring out of the speakers, it was as if God Himself wrapped His arms around me. A comforter for my frozen world. When I got to #9, *Hold On, Don't Let Go*. It's like God gave the artist the words of this song for me and my life. The chorus became the song I would sing to Jaden right before I had to leave him for the day. *Hold on, don't let go. Even though your heart hurts you so. He'll never let go of your hand.* This song became Jaden's lullaby.

My gospel playlist included songs like Whitney Houston's *I Love the Lord* and *Job's Song* by Hezekiah Walker. Kirk Franklin's *My Life is in Your Hands*, *More than I Can Bear*, and *He Will Take the Pain Away*. *I Won't Complain* by Reverend Paul Jones, *My Soul is Anchored* by Douglas Miller and *Let It Rain* by Bishop Paul Morton all became a lifeline to God's love despite my anguish.

It felt like God knew I wasn't feeling Him or His love through people. That their words were cement for the wall I was creating between us. He reminded me of His music. Knowing that the songs of His love, even in my despair was always my ladder out of the pit. I found myself, through my tears and heartache, praising God for who He is and the blessings I could still thank Him for.

Thanking Him for Khalil, although Khalil was no longer here. I learned how to give my pain to God and find comfort in Him who is able. I praised the God of my salvation. Forgiver of my sins. I'd walk through the rooms of my home crying Hallelujah until my voice refused to work. I started getting stronger. Strength to make it through the day. Then, I would become terrified that God would mistake my thanks as a thank you that Khalil was gone. I needed God to know that was *NOT* what I was thanking Him for. If I had it my way, I would still be pregnant until their August due date. And if I still had them, Khalil would not be dead, but in an incubator next to his brother.

As I praised, I would give God my disclaimer that I wanted Khalil to be alive, but I thanked Him for blessing me with him anyhow. Looking up to the Heavens and envisioning Khalil happy and smiling because he was in Heaven's Nursery. Imagining him cradled in the fluffiest clouds. *Something I envision even now whenever I marvel at the clouds. Wondering if the older kids are the ones making shapes because mine are too young to do so.*

The Kids Visit

On Memorial Day, I figured the strict rules would be lifted for me to take the kids to visit with Jaden since they have never been. I called and received permission that they could visit with the knowledge that it wouldn't be a long stay. Kamar's dad had no issue with bringing him back early for this trip.

Kamar was amazed at all we had to do before entering the room. Wash our hands, gown up, cover our heads and shoes, then wash our hands again. I explained that absolutely no germs could get in the room to make the babies even sicker than they already were.

After everyone was suited up, I took them in to see their brother. The mask over his eyes was gone as well as the cap on his head. The hole in his heart closed on its own and he was able to take in 1 ¾ ounces of milk. He still had tubes in his mouth and stomach, along with various IV's in his arms and feet. He was now dealing with NEC or Necrotizing Enterocolitis. This is when the intestinal wall is inflamed and infected. The reason why his stomach was almost bigger than his body. As they stroked his hand and talked to him, Jaden smiled the whole time. The doctor that delivered the twins was on that day and came in to tell Kamar something important.

"Did you know your brother Khalil was a superhero?"
Kamar's eyes lit up as he asked "How?"
"Did your mom tell you that Khalil had some deformities? Do you know what that means?" "Yes. She told me that his ear was a spiral and that his nose didn't go in the direction like mine."
"Yes. He knew that he was about to die because his liver and kidneys weren't functioning right. He knew that if he died in your mommy, Jaden would die also from shared infection. They shared everything in your mommy because they were identical twins. He didn't want Jaden to die, and he pushed him out of your mom saving his life. Isn't that what a superhero does?"

With tears in his eyes, Kamar turned back to Jaden and told him how much he wishes he could have seen Khalil and that he loved them both very much. This tore my already shattered heart because I had no pictures of Khalil, and I didn't think to have Kamar brought to the hospital to see him before his body was sent for cremation. Out of the three biggest regrets in my life. Not having a camera and not having him brought to the hospital to see his brother are the top two. *Not pledging Alpha Kappa Alpha Sorority Inc. when I had the chance is the third.*

It was now time to go. I had each of the kids tell Jaden bye and that they loved him. Jaden made a sound for the first time. He never made a sound during all my previous visits, which made this special. It lasted a millisecond and mimicked an 'ah.'

As we walked home, Kamar talked about his brother the superhero that he wished he could have met. I took them for ice cream because they were so happy they finally got to see their brother. That night was the first night since coming home from the hospital that I went to bed and slept.

At 1:22 am, NICU called to tell me Jaden passed away.

At first, I thought they had the wrong baby. I needed them to tell me where his incubator was located to prove to me they had the right baby. The doctor was very patient as I asked several times for confirmation that it was my baby that died.

Once I realized that it was in fact Jaden whom they were calling about, I woke the kids up and called Chase. To my surprise, he was sleeping in his car at the end of our block. Then I called my mother. In fifteen minutes, Chase, my mom and kids piled in a cab to see Jaden for the last time.

The kids Kamar (8), Autumn (2) and Teagan (1) were quiet during the ride. My tears fell on Teagan's cheek and Chase's fell on Autumn's. Kamar's tears found their resting place on my hand. As we reached the hospital and exited the cab, the driver saw our faces and said, "sorry for your loss." We walked into the hospital through a light rain. No need to suit up. Each child held and kissed their brother and got a picture with him.

Jaden did hold on. He held on for forty-one days and didn't let go until he saw his siblings.

To everyone that has ever donated to the blood bank, THANK YOU. It is because of people like you who gave us those days with him.

Glitches in Sanity

Jaden's memorial was held on the first Sunday in June after our regular service.

Afterwards, everyone came back to my apartment. Chase returned with us. It was then that I saw the extent of his mental break. He was sullen and unable to form complete sentences. He had severe tremors from all the medication his body was adjusting to. He was like a grown-up child asking if he could get something to eat, to asking if he could use the restroom. Evidence of a mental crisis was all in his demeanor.

Mine was stashed away in a corner of my mind. Its voice shouting in my head that sex with Chase would get me pregnant again and the boys would get reborn. But the act had to take place now. Jaden's spirit was on its way to be with Khalil. Sex with their dad would pull them both back redirecting them to me. It had to be now or never. Once we had sex, I would become immediately pregnant, and time would be reversed. These people had to leave.

I told my mom I needed to lay down, that I needed some quiet time. She got everyone to leave and took the kids home with her. I asked Chase to stay, but he said he needed to go to his aunt's house and would come back over. When he didn't come back and ignored my calls, I cried thinking I would never have the opportunity to place them back in me. They were gone forever.

The next morning, I felt that same urge again. To replace the babies that were dead, I had to have sex with Chase sometime during the midnight hour and I must rub their ashes over my belly for re-entry. I didn't like that idea of tampering with their ashes but was willing to do what needed to be done. At this point, I haven't even opened the containers to view the ashes *that would come years later*. I called Chase begging him to come over. When he asked what the emergency was, I couldn't tell him. I just asked, "Do I really needed a reason seeing at how both our sons are gone?" Besides, it wouldn't work if I told him. I asked my mom to keep the kids one more night for me and she agreed. Time was slipping and Chase hadn't come over yet. I eyed the boy's urns but couldn't bring myself to open them in case it jinxed the process. Chase just had to come through.

I paced and called. No answer. I started getting frantic. The voice in my head was screaming that it had to get done. Wondering if it would work with any guy if Chase did not show. No, was the answer given. The twins belonged to Chase, and he was the only one who could put them back. Finally, he came over but acted like he didn't know if he could perform. He said he would have to ask his therapist. I was enraged. Midnight was soon approaching, and I wasn't sure of our window of time. I couldn't tell him what needed to be done to get our boys back because I needed it to work. I needed my boys back in me.

As he sat on the sofa, he did not move when I removed his penis and started to perform oral. There was no penial reaction. He seemed to enjoy it, but not enough for an erection. Something he said was a side effect of one of the medications. Alarms were going off in my head. I sat on the other end of the sofa crying until I fell asleep. When I awoke in the morning, a blanket was over me and Chase was gone. I was hysterical wondering how long I was alone with the phone. What if the hospital called about Jaden? Then I remembered, Jaden had already passed away. I hated Chase all over again.

Kamar was going through it also. I was blind to how losing his brothers was affecting him. We were walking home one day when he ran in front of an oncoming car. Thank God he wasn't hit. As I went into the street and yelled at him asking "what the hell are you doing?" The driver got out to see if he was ok. With his eyes filling with tears, he told me in a calm and determined tone, "I wanted to talk to God to ask Him to return my brothers. I wanted them back from God." I picked my big baby up and held him as we sat on the stoop. I explained that his actions would leave me with no sons. That I needed him. I held him as he cried. I too wanted to cry but was dumbfounded by his grief. Questioning why I missed this? Failing my baby boy.

This was too much for me to handle on my own. Was this why he was asking me, "Was I was sure they were with God? Did God really hear his prayers? Does God really answer prayers? Can you talk to God?" The same little boy who once thought our Pastor was God, was now trying to die to see Him. I called my mother and his father seeking their help. It wasn't his father's weekend, but he came to get him anyway. Until then, my mom would talk it out with him. The urgency to replace the boys increased. Not just for my sake anymore. I became mentally occupied with trying to think of ways to get my twins back.

I started contemplating kidnapping a set of twins, weighing the pros and cons. The pros were that I could have babies for Kamar to be a big brother too. I would tell everyone that the hospital made a mistake. That my boys were given to another mom erroneously and they corrected their wrongdoing. This made perfect sense to me. The hard part would be finding a set of identical twin boys that were about five to six weeks old. I could even take some newborns. They would be small enough to resemble growing preemies.

As I took the kids to school and daycare, I was on the lookout for identical twin boys. If I had to kill the parent to do it, so be it. I started carrying around a butcher knife so I would be prepared. I was consumed. Rationalizing my plan with the opposing voices in my head. Even played with the idea of taking girls and just saying the sonograms were wrong. That thought didn't last though because my boys died. Not girls. Kamar already had living sisters, and he was wanting his brothers back. I also considered taking individual babies and raising them as twins. But trying to spot single babies was a hard task because they would need to look the same.

After a few days of unsuccessfully finding the babies I needed, I asked myself if I would be willing to take them in utero from another woman. It has been done before. Immediately, I felt the horror and sadness that I always felt when hearing those types of crimes. I became afraid of my own thoughts. Afraid of myself and what I had become.

The determination I had seeking other babies terrified me. Fearful of what I might do if I kept thinking like this. Would I really put that kind of pain on another mother? No. I couldn't be that person. Didn't want to be that person. I prayed for the devil to leave my mind and for God to cleanse it.

When I think about my thoughts on baby replacement, I pray for all the mothers out there who were denied the chance to raise their babies due to death. My prayer is for God to restore their minds before they act on thoughts of replacing an infant or child with one that belongs to another. That they do not deny themselves their grief but also find a way to hold on to God's love amid their hurt and pain.

Eventually Chase came over and spent the night. I took the time he was spending with the kids trying to do pregnancy calculations in my head. The chance to have Jaden and Khalil back in me was gone the next night after the memorial. However, maybe the new babies would be their reincarnations. I wanted to try. Again, Chase was not being sexually cooperative. He did come to bed with me, but I woke up by myself.

In the kitchen, as I was searching for the large knife to cut up some apples to go with the kids' breakfast, I asked Chase if he saw it. Without a word, he left and came back with it. With one hand on the knife and his arm around my waist, he leaned in close to ensure the kids didn't hear.

"The voices in my head saw you sleeping and questioned how you could sleep when you killed our boys. They told me if they had to die then so did you. I went and got the knife. I straddled over you holding it over your head with the voices telling me to kill you. You were asleep and they were dead. It wasn't fair for you to be sleeping. I held the knife over you while fighting the voices. Then I noticed that you were crying. Your tears shut the voices out and I got off you. Not trusting myself, I put the knife in the car."

I stood there in awe. Thinking that this nigga just told me voices in his head told him to kill me! This motherfucker was certified crazy. It was scary and hypocritical for me to be upset. I started laughing and soon my laughter gave way to tears. All I could say was that "after Khalil died, I prayed for your death. Didn't care how it happened, I just wanted you dead. Then Jaden died, and I wanted the boys back that I also took a mental detour. I understand why some women kidnap babies."

Looking in his eyes and thinking of Kamar's rational, I called the kids in the kitchen for an impromptu prayer circle.

I prayed right then for God to take away all thoughts that were unholy to Him. For Him to strengthen and comfort us. With amen said and before Kamar could go back into his room, I told him.

"Your brothers are our angels, forever with us. We are never going to get them back. Instead, when you feel an unexplainable warmth that only you feel, that is a hug and kiss from them. We will mourn, cry, get angry and miss them and that is normal. We have every right to feel every emotion because it is ours to feel. We just can't stay long in the bad emotions because angels are happy. They want us to be happy."

After a long hug, I wiped his tears and gave him kisses. Stroking his face, I told him that he is still the best big brother ever.

Time is an Oxymoron

With my sanity back in check, the focus returned to reality. I was back to being aware of the hurt and pain caused by the twins passing. Emotions so unbearable that I knew God was keeping me going because I just wanted to disappear. To not be seen for several days or even weeks. A place where there were no children who needed to be mothered. It may sound weird since I just cremated two of my babies, but I craved being alone with my grief. I didn't cry around the kids because I felt I had to be strong for them.

To escape, the kids and I went to stay at my sister's out of New York since Chase did not move back in. In hindsight, it probably was not the best decision. Why may you ask? Because even there, my grief had to be held at bay. I can remember only two times I couldn't hold it in. The first time we (my sis and mom) were in her car heading to the store and as she was parking, a gospel song I never heard before (nor again) played on the radio. The singer mentioned the emotions associated with the death of a baby and I broke down. They left me in the car for quality time with my tears. Watching them walk away talking felt as if my grief was mine and mine only. That they didn't care. I wanted them to stay and be silent. Instead, they made me feel more alone.

The second time, my sister and I were coming from McDonald's when I got call from my landlord letting me know he had to evict us. Because I didn't go to work for two months, the rent went unpaid for two months. When I spoke to him about the situation, he advised me that since we had paid a two-month rent deposit, he would use that money for May and June. He was sympathetic and allowed us two extra weeks in July to move out. She left me alone in the car to cry it out. I returned to Brooklyn leaving the kids there.

I loved being home by myself. I could sit talking to my boys boxed urns without the feeling of being judged. When I did this at my sister's, I was told it was unhealthy, and I needed to start moving on. They didn't understand that it was no different from going to a cemetery and talking to the dead at your feet and laying flowers. My dead just happen to be in arms reach. *Let me say for the first four years after their death, I took their urns with me whenever we traveled. I was not ready to leave them alone.*

I would stroke the tops of the boxes as if it was their head. Something I still do. Just reaching out and running my hand along the top with a whisper of I love you, good morning, good night or just a simple, "I miss you boys."

I would sit them in whatever room I was packing in, having a one-way conversation between myself, God, and the boys. I was still angry and seeking a deeper understanding of my current situation. But in the quietness, where the only other sounds were songs of God's love in the background. Somewhere between the tears and pain, I would lift my hands in praise.

It was in these moments I believe that Jesus and I started renewing our relationship. In the middle of packing as I went into worship while mourning, a sensation would radiate from my heart filling me with an unexplainable, overwhelming sensation of gratitude for my Savior. All my heartache went away. Replaced with a combination of joy, peace and love that it feels like my soul is smiling, and my heart is mending.

Even my extreme hatred for Chase started to subdue. He was coming around to assist with packing the heavier boxes since I couldn't lift more than a few pounds. He had adjusted his meds and was on a regimen that provided glimpses of his old self. An old self that was still a mystery to me because that too was a medicated version.

One evening, I disassembled Teagan's crib that the boys were going to use. As the tears rolled down my face, I carried the pieces out for trash pickup. I'm sure I looked a mess when I opened the front door to the outside carrying pieces of a demolished future in my hands.

The door was held open for me and through my tears I mumbled a thank you. I saw pity in her eyes. The woman she was speaking to also saw me and must have taken that as a queue to speak louder. With each step, I heard her talk about the healthiness of her twin daughters. Of how they would be coming home from the hospital in just a few days. Like she wanted me to hear. I didn't even know she was pregnant and pregnant with twins at that. *I think God hid this from me during my mental hiatus.*

When I laid the frame of the crib on the sidewalk, it felt as if I was placing caskets on the ground. Burying the life of my boys. Her words of healthy babies bouncing off the shattered remnants of my heart. As I passed her to go back upstairs to retrieve the mattress, I heard, "I am so lucky to have both my babies alive." I never spoke to this woman to cause her to be so unkind.

In a cloud of grief, I went upstairs and laid on the infant mattress and cried. As I cried, I got angry. I called my mother to tell her what just happened and between sobs, I told her I couldn't go back outside. My reason was because if she was still out there and started shouting about her baby girls, I didn't think the police would arrest me for assault.

She told me, "Nothing else needs to go out tonight. Don't let the ignorance of others cause you to be violent." I started to follow her instructions, but the more I thought about it, the angrier I got. I cleaned my face and took more pieces of the crib out hoping she would be there. I wanted her to be there. I wanted to release my rage upon her. God knew this, so when I opened the door, the stoop was empty.

The next day when Chase came over, I told him what happened, and he took charge of disposing the rest of the crib, mattress and whatever baby items that Teagan didn't use anymore. I felt like my life was shattering more day by day. Worship helped me forget in that moment, but it didn't alter my reality. Eviction, panic attacks, disappointments and grief. I didn't know what to do or where to turn.

And that brings me to two situations that happened at work.

When I found out that one of my co-workers just had a son, I brought him an unopened gift set of a onesie with matching hat, booties and burp cloth. When I gave it to him, the compassion and sadness he had for me was all over his face and too much for me to handle. I went back to my desk and cried. I needed more work to focus on and asked for it. They were hesitant but obliged.

With more of my responsibilities coming back to me, I thought I would be strong enough to take care of a matter that arose.

I received a letter from the hospital instructing me to bring Jaden in for routine bloodwork since he had several transfusions. All that night and in the morning, I thought about how I was going to lay it into them for this preposterous request. And I did.

I made the call from my desk, laughing at the horrible record keeping of the hospital. I let them have it. "How do you not know that the baby you are asking for is no more? That it is impossible for me to get blood from ashes!" I was fine during that whole conversation. Even laughed about it.

Shortly after hanging up the phone, the request and my inability to fulfill it hit me like a dump truck dropping its load onto my chest. I couldn't breathe. I was sweating and became nauseous. I went to the bathroom and threw up until all I could do was gag. Some of my co-workers came in with me. They wiped my forehead with a wet napkin and kept my hair out of my face. When they suggested to call an ambulance, I told them I wanted to go to the Cathedral on the corner.

I was weak and crying, yet not in myself. I say that because I saw from the outside what was happening. I saw two people on both sides of me holding me up. A limp body where the only sounds emitting were dry cries. I saw people in the office standing and watching, some were crying themselves. I saw the elevator come and stop on the 14th floor and four people enter. Upon exiting on the 1st floor, I heard someone say, "We got her. Her twins died so we are taking her to the church. She will be fine there." They placed me in the pew and waited with me until I found my voice enough to ask to be alone.

I sat in that beautiful Catholic Cathedral, with its' lit candles and stained-glass windows. It was so quiet that I found peace in the silence of the sanctuary. I let stillness comfort me. Feeling God's presence all around me. Feeling as if my twins were with me. Time was of no essence, so I don't know how long I sat there. When I felt strong enough, I took the train and headed home. I didn't go to work the next day.

The Power of a Game

With all my remaining things placed in storage, we handed over the keys to the landlord. I went to moms to stay since she was still with my sister, and Chase went to a friends place.

A few days in, my cousin Carlos invited me to start over in North Carolina. He talked it over with his wife and the two of them decided I should come and stay with them and their two kids in their three-bedroom apartment. When he brought this to me, it was all laid out. Their kids would share a room, and me and my kids could have the other room. They would put down an air mattress for the kids, and I could sleep on the bed that was in there. I asked him for a few days to give him an answer.

I first ran this by Xavier since this would directly affect him and Kamar's weekends together. He was not happy at first and we discussed Kamar going to live with him. The demands of his job would make it impossible, so he gave me permission for our son to go with me.

I then bought this to my mom and sister who agreed with Xavier. It hurt to tell TT I was leaving for the South with her great grands. Her health was not doing well making it hard to leave her. She provided me with something that I desperately needed to leave. Her blessing and confidence that everything would be ok.

The only person that was not on board with this decision was Chase. When I asked him to give me another option, he couldn't. The kids and I were not welcome to stay with him, and he did not have a job or savings to provide for us. And there wasn't even an us anymore.

I set a date of two weeks to leave Brooklyn and handed in my notice at work.

That first week at my mom's, Chase picked me up from the train station and had dinner with me. As we ate, I would look at him with mixed emotions. Hating him while having sympathy for him. To pass the time and ignore the tension, we would play Scrabble. He had medicated more of his demons (as he would say) to the point that he was the same man I met on that warm September day. Just a tad bit more reserved due to his grief. After dinner, as we finished the game, he'd go back to his friend's leaving me alone and with nothing to do.

That first weekend, he came over in the morning, and we spent the day playing multiple games of Scrabble. Just like every night, as we pondered over words to create, we talked. It was in those conversations that the tension eased. That Saturday night was the first time we made love. Grief interrupted us before either of us could climax. We laid wrapped in each other's arms and cried over the detour life brought us. Over our decrease in numbers. Over the fact that I was moving the kids away and there was nothing he could come up with to stop me.

At the start of the last week on the job, he would walk me to the train station in the morning and be there when I got off. Then dinner, Scrabble and then he'd leave. That Thursday my co-workers took me to lunch with well wishes for a healing future. I printed all the emails of the announcements of the birth and death of my boys. Goodbye emails and keep in touch ones. I never did. I knew all they would remember was that I was the employee whose twins had died. I made that day my last.

On Friday, during a game of Scrabble while we ate breakfast, we decided not to stay indoors. We headed to Coney Island to sit on the beach and watch the waves. We packed for our trip. Just taking towels to sit on for neither of us wanted to go into the water.

On the train ride there, if you looked at us, we were just another couple. Sitting together holding hands lost to our own worlds. It was the same way on the beach looking out at the water. Watching people enjoy the relief of the hot sun by wave jumping. Although there were a lot of people there, it was peaceful. At times you could hear the waves crash over the noise.

At some point, staring out at the water next to Chase, I heard a voice whisper that my boys were out on the water. I asked Chase if he heard it and he did not. I heard it several more times before becoming mesmerized enough to get up and walk towards the water.

Mommy. Mommy.
They are right out there. All you need to do to see them is go out in the water.
I don't see them.
You must go out further. Don't you hear them calling for you?
Mommy. Mommy.
Don't you want to see your sons?
Mommy. Mommy.
Are you going to abandon them? Come in further.
I can't swim.
They are crying for you. Don't you hear them?
Mommy we want to see you. Come and get us.

The water is waist high, but I keep my balance.

Mommy. Mommy.
They need you. Go see your sons.
Your boys are not out there.
They are! They're beyond the horizon waiting for you.
Don't go any further or you're going to drown. Stand still. Do you see anything except the ocean?

Mommy. Mommy.
They are waiting for you. Come.
If you go out there, you are going to die.
No, you won't. You will be able to see your boys.
Stand still and listen. I want you to turn back. Your boys are in heaven with the Father. You have three other children who need their mother.

Something in me breaks and I turn back to where Chase is. I search for him and spot him. I am surprised I am so far out. Be it for the grace of God I never lost my footing. Never fell in the water. My feet were planted although the sand was always shifting. I made it back to shore without a struggle. When I sat down next to Chase, he didn't even notice I was gone. He asked when I went into the water.

I didn't explain anything. I sat staring at the water going over what I just went through. Analyzing what I heard and who could I have heard it from? Was my mind playing tricks on me again? Scared and unable to speak, I laid on his shoulder not wanting him to know how emotional I was. Never telling him what just happened. I thanked God for coming into the mental conversation and for breaking through the stronghold of deceit.

When we got back to my mom's place, we showered together and went back out to pick up Chinese food. After a game of Scrabble, we made love with the intensity of two hurting people struggling to forget our reality. The reality that our time together was coming to an end. That our family would never be the same. That the next chapter of our lives were headed in two different directions. I forgave Chase that night for leaving me emotionally, physically and mentally broken by not being by my side when I needed him the most. For not being the man, I expected and needed him to be when it mattered the most.

BOOK THREE

Not in Brooklyn Anymore

When the time came, the kids and I boarded the Amtrak headed for North Carolina.

Amongst our bags that we carried were the ashes of Jaden and Khalil. As the train pulled into our destination, the realization that I was there because of their death ladened me with sadness. Was it a new start? A change of scenery? Or was I running away? No matter how I looked at it, I went from living with Chase and the kids in our own place, to moving in with my cousin and his family.

From being pregnant with twins, to carrying their urns.

It was an adjustment to say the least. Carlos and his family were great. For them to open their home to us was a blessing. Having access to a washer, dryer, and dishwasher all in the home was new. No more laundromats and having to wash dishes when I didn't want to quickly spoiled me. Between the pool, playground, and basketball court on the premises, the kids stayed entertained.

I found myself unable to sleep most nights because of the quietness. I started watching the show *COPS* to fall asleep. The sounds of sirens and yelling became the lullaby of the life I left, guiding me to sleep.

As the only smoker, out on their balcony, I used the time to be alone with my thoughts. My grief was limited to cigarette breaks. I did not want them to regret inviting us if I was always a walking, crying mess. I allowed myself to acknowledge my heartbreak only on the balcony with a cigarette in hand talking to God. *Cigarette smoke stinks, so for them to allow me this necessity was appreciated.*

I couldn't be lazy and depressed. I had to find a job and learn how to drive. Carlos gave me lessons and only one time did life pass in front of us. I took the turn into the complex on two wheels in his jeep. After the jeep safely came out of the lean and went back on all four wheels did we remember to breathe. We both needed a beer after that lesson.

I got Kamar enrolled in school, and the girls at a local church's daycare. I found employment at a store in the nearby shopping center. My body was still healing from the delivery, so doing a lot of bending and standing was not pleasing to my back. One day the supervisor instructed me to put a small bookcase together for the display of various fragrances.

"I'm sorry but I am not good at following directions which is why I have five kids out of wedlock." She didn't laugh.
"Well, this is a simple bookcase and shouldn't be a problem."
"I tried to put a small nightstand together once and built it backwards and had to start over."
"You will be fine. It's in the back."

I go to the back, take a look and decide that I'm not going to do this. I go back out to find her.

"I'm sorry. I saw the bookcase and for me to put it together will be a strain on my back so I'm going to have to decline."
"Wait? Are you telling me no? You won't follow my instruction?"
"Politely, yes. I cannot do it."

And with that, I was fired. I really couldn't do it. My back took most of the trauma from my hospital stay and was slowly recovering. If I remember correctly, I held that job for less than a month. Truth be told, I found that working was difficult. People want to know about you. They asked questions about your life, your accent and why you moved. I did not prepare myself for that and tried to answer as vaguely as possible by stating, "I just wanted a new start."

The question that always tormented me when asked if I had kids. If I answered three, then I felt as if I was denying my boys. If I answered five, then say that two were in Heaven's Nursery, it made me want to disappear into my sorrow. I didn't want to make them uncomfortable, nor did I know how to handle the sympathy of strangers.

By the time Thanksgiving came around, I was broke, unemployed and still living with my cousins. Kamar's dad had to work and thought it was best for us to stay together with this being the first holiday since our lives changed.

My son and I were both having a difficult time and we talked it out. We were the only two carrying pain. I was trying to hide my depression from him and everyone else. This bottled-up intense sadness manifested itself into a nightmare that thankfully only came one time. Unfortunately, I can recall every difficult detail.

I'm back at my desk explaining to the nurse at the hospital why I couldn't bring Jaden in for bloodwork. Instead of sympathy and apologies like I received with that phone call, this nurse had no patience. She hurriedly informed me that there was a mix-up.

"The bloodwork isn't for testing him. It was a blood transfusion for Jaden. There is also a special type of blood available for Khalil." I explained again that neither one would be able to receive blood nor give blood because they were dead.

"No dear," she says. "You are not understanding me. This blood will give them life. All you must do is bring their bodies in. You have their bodies, don't you? Put their bodies in a Tupperware container and bring them in. We will give them this transfusion, and you will be able to hold your baby boys. Wouldn't that be nice? To hold them and kiss them and watch them grow. Just bring them in by 1 a.m. or the blood will not work."

I find my voice to tell her that they are dead.

"Well, you buried them, didn't you? Dig them up and bring them in. This blood will give them life."
"I had them cremated. They are nothing but ashes."
"That's all right dear. Our team of specialists will be able to put them together, so they can have life. Your boys weren't dead in the first place. Just in a deep sleep."

"They are not buried but cremated." I scream.

"Are you telling me you thought those precious babies were dead? What kind of mother are you? You killed them in the fire. Well, now we will need them here within the hour. I'll hold while you dig them up. You buried them, didn't you?"

I place the phone on a mound of dirt and can hear the nurse telling me I have an hour. I am no longer in business clothes at my desk. Instead, I am in the same jeans and T-shirt I first met Chase in, including the battered red Old Navy hat on my head. I am on my knees digging in dirt with my hands trying to retrieve their boxes. She keeps repeating that they were just asleep, not dead. As I am digging, I see the boxes and yell, "I have them!"

But they slip out of my hands and fall deeper. The red cap falls off my head and turns to blood pulsating with life flowing downward towards the boxes that keep falling deeper every time the tips of my fingers touch them. I am crying because I hear the nurse say they are not dead, just in a deep sleep and she is counting down the time I have left to bring them in.

I am screaming to her that "I want my boys back, but they keep falling!" Crying. Screaming. Digging. Falling.

On repeat until someone wakes me up because I am verbalizing all this loudly.

Later that day, my cousin's wife asked to see the box that holds every piece of their existence. She took her time reading through emails, cards, looking at photos of Jaden in the incubator and of him deceased. Their certificates and hospital bracelets. She got emotional going through everything.

Her request made me feel like she was acknowledging the moments they lived. And in that space, for the first time, I did not feel alone.

New Address

Chase had found employment in Brooklyn and wanted to help by cutting a check directly to the daycare. This was an appreciated parental move, but after the fourth bounced check, the girls got expelled when I couldn't come up with the outstanding fees.

Now, to make the price drop, I could have joined the church the daycare was at, but when I visited a regular Sunday service, it wasn't my cup of tea. I don't like churches where at the end of service, they take up an offering asking for specific dollar amounts. Special occasion services are fine, but if this was happening at a regular service, then this is just how they operate. I also could have tried my hand at getting assistance, but I didn't. Even now I don't know why? I think I called shortly after coming to the state and was rejected because I wasn't there for more than six months, nor did I have my own address.

By December, I found a job through a temp agency more aligned with my skills. I went to work for a supply company working in accounts receivable. It wasn't far from my cousins, which was good because I relied on them to get to and from work. Not only was I hiding my grief, but I was also hiding the feelings of self-hatred from being independent in Brooklyn, to becoming a burden in Raleigh.

But again, I put on a happy face. My children, especially Kamar, needed me to put on this mask. I felt my cousins needed it too.

As tax season rolled in, my temporary status on the job changed to permanent. While Carlos shopped in Walmart, I had my taxes done. As the preparer was having me sign the last set of documents, the fact that Khalil and Jaden could both be claimed sent me over the edge I was teetering on. They could be claimed because they were born with a heartbeat. They both breathed. Even though they died, they lived.

When Carlos came over to me. I couldn't form words. The tax preparer told him what set me off. The questions of why they had to die glared from a neon sign in my head, breaking the damn of tears that were mainly free to fall during smoke breaks on the balcony or on Sunday's during service.

With the permanent status on the job, and a tax refund of over $6,000 *last time I saw that much*, I moved into a two-bedroom, two-bathroom apartment in the same complex.

I gave the girls the master suite and Kamar had the other bedroom. I slept on an air mattress in the dining room until I could get my things out of storage in Brooklyn. I bought my first car and was also able to give my cousins a little thank you money.

I was becoming established. I was independent again. I could cry while fixing dinner if I wanted to. I could talk freely and openly with the kids about their brothers. We could grieve together as a family. But most importantly. The boys could come out of the bag they were in and take their spot out in the open with their family. We placed them on the mantel over the fireplace with white candles on each side. We had our own place to call home.

Mommy Dearest

Having a place for just me and the kids was great after spending eight months living with Carlos and his family.

We started finding a rhythm to life in the Carolinas. As the days turned into weeks, emotionally, things started falling apart for me. Homesickness for Brooklyn was growing strong. With no friends to hang out with, loneliness engulfed me. Tears lulled me to sleep almost every night.

A co-worker invited me to her church in Southeast Raleigh. There, I found a new hospital for my soul.

Crying for the turn my life had taken. Grieving for the death of my twins. Questioning if I had made the right decision to stay in NC knowing that it took Kamar away from weekends with his dad. Then leaving church, before we could even pull off the grounds, I would be yelling and cursing at the kids in anger. Becoming disgusted with myself for yelling and cursing at them, being all mean when I had just finished praising God in service.

Trying to pinpoint what was causing this shift almost every Sunday. A shift that I didn't experience when I lived with my cousins and spent the service crying at their church. Then, returning home without an outlet for these unstable emotions except by smoking. But even the cigarettes didn't help. They calmed me down, yes. However, the real reason for smoking was it gave me a chance to be alone.

After several weeks of attending church and turning into a monster on the way home, emotional stress took the form of a nightmare.

I'd be sleeping when a black shadowy figure stood over me and calmly told me, "Wake up! Your kids are dead." I would get up and see the kids through a hazy film, sleeping and say, "It was just a dream," and lay back down.

Then the figure would say, "It's not a dream. Kamar, Autumn and Teagan are dead. Wake up!" Again, I would go and check to make sure this was not true. When I looked at them, the room was still hazy, and they looked like dolls. I'd go back to bed saying to myself that it was just a dream, they aren't dead.

The figure would appear again saying, "Your kids are now dead!" I would wake up in a sweat with my heart beating fast and my breathing labored. Realizing that I was just awaking from a dream, I would go into their rooms to make sure each one of them was breathing. This time, there wasn't a cloudy wall of air in the way I saw them. It was with clarity that I saw their chest rising and falling indicating life.

This dream confused and scared the hell out of me. Each time I woke up seemed so real that I was having a hard time grasping that although I woke up and got out of bed when the figure told me too, I was still asleep. Asleep each time I checked on them which is why they looked like dolls, and the room was never clear until I finally truly woke up and went into their rooms.

The frequency of this dream that I penned the 3-tiered dream since I was "waking up" three times was happening so often that I became afraid of going to sleep. This dream was not pleasant. It was feeding the fear of losing my remaining children. After tucking them in at night, I would spend the rest of the time periodically checking on them to make sure they were still breathing. Fearful that if I did go to sleep, they would die. I would lie on my air mattress tossing and turning then getting up to check on them.

When I did sleep, the same scenario would play out, and I would not be able to go back to sleep even after checking on them. If I went to sleep and didn't have the dream, but woke up to use the bathroom, before I could lay back down, I would check on them two or three times. If the girls were sleeping with me, the figure would be standing over them telling me they were dead. If all the kids were in the living room sleeping, the dream would still come. If we were at my sisters, I would still have the dream. It didn't matter where we were, the nightmare traveled with me.

Because of this, Kamar ended up being late to school almost every morning and I was written up for the number of times I was late. How could I explain that a 3-tiered dream that woke me up even though I was still asleep, was keeping me awake at night? That sometimes, depending on the time it occurred, would keep me up for additional hours before exhaustion took over and put me back to sleep that I didn't hear my alarms go off? It would sound like an elaborate excuse and not my life.

I went to see a doctor about this and was prescribed sleeping pills. The first night I took them, Kamar woke me up because Teagan was screaming and crying. I realized I couldn't take them due to the deep sleep they caused. I felt as if I was losing my sanity. To make matters worse, an incident occurred that frightened me. I had a wet dream that was all too real. It included pain in my vaginal area, panties down around the ankles and my shirt off. So real that I got up to see if someone had come into the apartment and had their way with me. Even smelled my fingers to find out if it was me. It wasn't.

As the months came and went. I was on my third write-up for lateness. It didn't matter that my work was impeccable. I instituted new processes that the department adopted that decreased collections and streamlined credit card disputes. My arrival time was about fifteen minutes late and that was the issue.

Personally, I think it had more to do with my evaluation of management and how they executed the mentality of the good 'ole boys club. Nevertheless, the next day I was three minutes late and was let go the week before Christmas. Hello unemployment my old friend.

Thoughts of suicide decided to move in and become roommates with the depression.

Who Am I?

Ideas of driving the car off a bridge as I approached it seemed easy.

Kamar would go and live with his father, and the girls would go to my sister. I knew that between her and his dad, the kids would still get to see each other. Ending my life would reunite me with my boys. Some of these thoughts involved the kids.

When I would think of having all my kids in Heaven with me, I would envision crashing into the trees at high speed. Then get a panic attack at the thought of any of the kids surviving. The amount of trauma I would have caused them. Growing up knowing they survived their mom trying to kill them. I did not want them to have to live with that so I would pray for God to take us via carbon monoxide. The figure that told me they were dead always showed them peaceful. I knew death would be kind to them.

I, on the other hand was proving to be a piss poor mother. My responses to my children were becoming more erratic. I was snapping at Kamar for the littlest things and then would feel terrible about it. This caused me to convince myself that they would be better off without me.

It seemed every time I became at peace with ending my life, I would get into an argument with my sister or his dad and decide that I didn't want anyone else to raise my kids. I knew that was God intervening on their behalf.

I didn't know who I was anymore though.

I didn't see me when I looked in the mirror. I didn't feel like me. What did I like? What didn't I like? What made me smile? When

I ask myself these things, I drew a blank. Did God take my boys because I was unfit? Was He working His way to the ones left by causing me to lose my mind? Crying in service and cursing in the car on the way home? Scared to sleep? What type of person did I become? Questioning what demons I was harboring to make me act this way?

This loss of identity reminded me of when I was a pre-teen, *can't remember the actual age and can't find the documents*. My mom wanted to change my last name to hers. See, at birth I was given TT's last name. Not even Lawrence's last name which was different from his mothers'.

When she asked me, I didn't know how to answer. My name was me. How I introduced myself. What other people called me by. I felt as if I said no, my mom would think I didn't love her. If I said yes, then TT would think I didn't love her. Terrified of losing love from both of them. There was no positive way to come out of this. *Thinking back, I should have asked to just hyphen the names.*

In the end, I went with my mom because of the pressure I felt.

I didn't feel as if I could talk to my family or friends because it seemed as if the boy's death didn't touch them. That with their death went any feelings whatsoever about them and the effect it caused. Because they never came home from the hospital, they weren't real.

I can recall one evening, my sister called crying telling me that she understood what I went through with Jaden. How do you wonder? From an episode of *Grey's Anatomy*. I too was watching that episode. That was, until they showed the baby in the incubator with all its tubes, then I had to turn it off. It was too real of a depiction of what Jaden went through. I was angry at her for this confession. That it took a tv show to show her what I was dealing with all those times she told me to "think of Job."

Several days after the first anniversary of their birth, I got the call that TT had left this earth. My grandmother. My love and my life. My TT was no longer a phone call away.

Grass Isn't Always Greener

To make the situation worse, *yes, it did get worse*. I was finding out that living in the South was not cheaper in every way than up north like I always heard it was.

When it comes to renting, you will definitely get space and amenities not found in New York for half the cost. In Brooklyn, it's easy to find a home daycare or two within a three-block radius. In NC, home day cares are few with more choices of store front daycare centers. Which are more expensive. Let me not even get into car payments, car insurance, and a $250 new driver stipend/penalty.

My expenses were slowly eating up my income and financial difficulties were starting to bang down my door.

After four months of sleeping on an air mattress, I received a call from the storage company that I had a week to come up with the past four months fees or everything would be auctioned off. This was my fault for trusting Chase to take care of this bill after what happened with daycare. I put my trust in him because: one - he was working and two - I needed the financial help.

I begged the storage company for an extra week after explaining the situation to them. Chase was able to secure a van and went to remove the items out of storage after the past dues' fees were paid. The only furniture that was in storage was the dining room set and the sectional. Other than that, it was mostly boxes. I stressed to him that the most important items were my boxes of photos, awards, yearbooks, and degree that were in three boxes labeled life. These boxes were needed in lieu of any furniture.

I would tell him, "Either the boxes and the sectional, or the dining set and the boxes. If you bring the boxes with all the photos of the kids, I'd be satisfied." Having photos from birth until we moved from Brooklyn meant a lot for me to have. *Remember, my mom had none of me as a baby.* He knew this and knew why it was important to have photos of their life from the moment they were in my arms in the hospital.

When he arrived with the van, my disappointment in finding only boxes of clothes along with the sectional and dining set was evident. He said, "There wasn't any room for more boxes."

I looked at him contemplating if this was done on purpose. Punishment for moving. The boxes I wanted more than anything had the word LIFE all over them. He knew this and knew how much it meant for me to have them back. I won't lie and say it wasn't nice to eat at a table and sleeping on the queen-sized sofa bed from the sectional. However, I was devastated that I lost all my babies' photos and items from my life to share with them. I prayed for God to reveal why I continued to put my trust in Chase when he already got me into a financial bind.

In need of a release and no one to provide it, my co-worker set me up a friend of hers. He came over one evening after the kids were asleep. We played Scrabble to make conversation easier. I flirted anticipating intercourse later. When he left after the game was over, I was confused. I stood there in a T-shirt and boy shorts asking why he was leaving.

"You are too aggressive, and I'm not used to that." I looked at him like he had lost his damn mind and asked him to explain. "You asked me to fuck and that if I won, I could choose where and how to have sex. Who does that."

As I locked the door behind him, I couldn't help but ask myself, "how that was aggressive?"

I was not meeting anyone. Granted, I only went to work, church, and stores which probably aided in the difficulty of meeting men. I also believe there was an aura of sadness that I carried with me that kept people away. In New York, I had a rolodex of guys I could call on. Never a shortage of them. Here in the South, it was making sense to me why so many people married the person they dated in school. Seemed to this city girl that was the only way to find someone.

Between the sexual frustration, unemployment, nightmares, lack of sleep and feeling an identity lost, suicidal thoughts became my daydreams. Losing my memories that were in storage didn't help either. There were other factors that were sending me on a downward spiral. I was desperate for some release. An escape away from me.

I remembered a guy that spent a summer with his dad in Brooklyn for a year. We hung out together the whole summer and then he never came back. Whenever I asked his dad about him, he would tell me that he lived in Raleigh and was doing well. I went to Facebook in search of him. When I found him and verified that he remembered the girl from his dads block that he hung out with for the summer that year, I asked him for a favor.

"I'm still new to the area and don't go out to meet people. Would you be kind enough to fuck me? I don't want a relationship, just need to get laid." I had to wait a few days, but he came through. The problem was that I got a taste of sex again and once was not enough. I became a stalker. Wanting to be with him all the time. Not because he was a nice guy or anything, he just had what I needed. A penis. It didn't even bother me that he snuck recorded me. I saw the camera on the stand and did not believe him when he said it wasn't on.

During my junior year at the university, I worked at a place that boosted being the only full nudity, girl on girl, bondage and domination establishment. I took the cash at the front and only filled in once when they were short on girls. I knew where to hide to take pictures and where to put the extra cameras management didn't want their customers to see. I knew all about camera placement, hiding it and leaving it out in the open. Most importantly, I know when the camera is on.

After a few times at either his place or mine, I stopped seeing him because I didn't like the neediness that I went after him with. I craved the way sex made me forget about my issues, just not with him.

By the early part of 2008, I had found employment again, and despite how much Chase hated NC, he came to live with us. The day after he moved in, he found a job working construction. This created a multitude of problems that I'm not sure where to start.

He still blamed me for our twins death, and I let him because I believed him. I blamed me too. It bothered me that there weren't many days he wouldn't remind me that it was my fault. If we were having sex, I tolerated it. We argued plenty and made up plenty. When we became pregnant again, the grief we were still in came back to the front of the line.

Emotions were once again raw, but this time, fueled by the fragile balance of love and hate. Berating and uplifting. Condemnation and support. If you think those things shouldn't go together, for us they did. Yet, we considered having this baby. That was until the next argument or tearful shouting match. After a week of feeling just as mental as him when he is off his meds, he went to have a vasectomy while I went to have an abortion. Neither of us was ready to have another baby to die on us. I didn't want to put my children through that again. I didn't feel as if I had the mental capacity for another death when my mind was still fragile.

These destructive behaviors were taking a toll.

There was one time we were arguing about Autumn pushing and biting kids at daycare. As he turned it back to the ban at the hospital, I noticed a silverfish crawling on the wall. I went to get bug spray and sprayed it. A few minutes later, Chase starts to motion that his throat is itching and closing.

Standing there, I was debating on what to do. Do I assist or do I let him die? Then I decide that I don't want to expose the kids to his dead body. I rush across the street to buy Benadryl. After drinking half the bottle, he starts to feel better. The next day at lunch, I go to the store and buy three more bottles of that same bug spray. When I knew he should be coming in, I sprayed the foyer emptying out one can. The moment he walks through the door, and starts to take off his shoes, he begins to cough and leaves. I think *maybe I should have waited a week instead of a day. Been out of Brooklyn for a short time and already forgot street law.*

By June, things between us became irreconcilable. Coming home after Kamar's 6th grade graduation, all his things were gone. He did not show up the next day for Autumn's graduation from daycare. He left without a word to me or the kids.

Life Goes On

I wasn't sad to see him go because his presence and arguing added additional disruption to our home. After a while, the kids stopped asking about him. All was well for a short spell.

Even though I found permanent employment, it didn't provide an income greater than my expenses. I was drowning in debt and self-loathing. I was evicted from the apartment complex in June of '09. Even with borrowing the rent from family and getting a rent grant from church, I could not stay. This eviction felt different from the one in Brooklyn after the boys died. It added to the feeling of hopelessness and helplessness that I was already in. Beating myself up for screwing up and losing our home. I was the definition of failure.

Employed eviction was hard to swallow. Knowing that I lost the shelter to provide for my children was beyond devastating. I felt like I was sitting at Satan's table. As I passed the chicken seasoned with my soul, he passed me despair. While I was packing for homelessness, I was unscrewing the legs of the dining room table when I lost my grip, and the table fell on my desktop keyboard that was on the floor. I hurried up and laid the table upside down *which is how I should have had it to remove the legs in the first place* and assessed the damage to the keyboard. Surprisingly there wasn't any.

I couldn't believe it. I thought the crunch I heard were several keys coming detached. That they would all fall to the floor when I picked it up and the keyboard itself would be in half. This intrigued me so I sat to think if it could mean anything. *I love symbolism.* I looked at the table falling as my current situation. The loss of grip on the table was the loss of grip in not losing our home. And although we had to move and had nowhere to go, it wouldn't break us (the keyboard). The resounding crunch of homelessness would be just that. A temporary sound. It may not look like it, but things will remain intact.

I started crying thanking God that it was the summertime, and the kids were not hip to what was going on since I sent them to my sisters for the summer and Kamar had left to go live with his dad permanently.

The topic of him moving came up one day after school. He experienced an erection during class. I told him when it happened again, to think of something gross like roaches in his food. I realized that I might not be the best person to take him through the journey of puberty. Thankfully, he had a dad in his life who wanted to chance to be a full-time dad.

The decision for him to go was a difficult one mainly for the fact that I didn't want to lose my only living son. The only other person who could talk with me about imagined futures of Jaden and Khalil. Letting him go meant that my failure as a mother was fact and not circumstantial emotions. I was fearful that he would think I didn't love him. We had the same temperament so we would bump heads a lot but then I never wanted my son to feel that I wasn't choosing him. I just knew the character of his father and thought it was best to let him take him into manhood. So, it was just me that needed shelter.

My cousins had just bought a house where I found myself staying for two weeks keeping my clothes in the car. A place to live had just been over the horizon.

My mother decided to relocate from Brooklyn. We moved into a three-bedroom, two-bathroom apartment. This is how my mom and I along with the girls became roommates. This new living arrangement took some adjustment.

Regression

Living with my mom made me feel like a child again. Sure, the circumstances were different, but I felt as if I couldn't live how I used to. For example, cleaning up on a Saturday morning listening to Eminem or the Notorious B.I.G while the girls were in their room because I knew she would find the language offensive.

I felt uncomfortable being me around her. It was either I cursed too much, used too much salt cooking or let the girls be little girls. I was no longer in control of my household because it was a shared one. We were roommates sharing the living expenses. I had been on my own for so long raising my kids that I didn't know how to live with my mother. A man, yes. My mom, no. I felt like I was retreating instead of growing.

I had to move the boys into my room because she was uncomfortable with the way the girls and I acknowledged them. I remember one time on their birthday; I sat with the girls going through their box. Talking about them while tears streamed down my face. She simply stated that I should move on and put that stuff away. This angered me because I was moving on. I was still living. It was just important for me that the girls do not forget they had baby brothers at one point in their life.

After several months of us living together, I was laid off due to the company being bought out. Thankfully I received a nice severance package, but being home out of work didn't help any.

Missing Kamar and seeing young boys in the stores that reminded me of my son and just wanting to hug them as if I was hugging him bought on a different kind of sadness. Often taking long walks in the neighborhood to clear my head. But until then, I needed a distraction.

He came in the form of a fast-food worker that I'll call Mr. Wendy's. He was breakfast eye candy and sometimes lunch. When I was working, my co-workers and I frequently ate there. I had a crush on this short muscular dark chocolate creation by God that I probably gained a few extra pounds making trips there just to get a view of him. When being out of work for several months started taking its toll, I went and saw Mr. Wendy's. It was my lucky morning because I caught him taking out the trash and asked.

"Are you married or in a relationship?"
"No. Why?"
"Because I was laid off some months ago and can't keep coming here to eat just to get a look at you."
"Oh word!"
"Don't be offended but you have this just out of prison look about you. Were you locked up?"
"(Laughing) Yeah. Did four years."
"Thought so. Here is my number, call or text and just say you are Mr. Wendy's. Not looking for a relationship, just some fun."

I walked away thinking that maybe I am aggressive. Or maybe I just know how quickly life can change, and don't have time to dance around what I want. When he did call, I let him know that I was only interested in a sexual acquaintance, and he was fine with that. He mainly stopped by on his lunch break during the week. If he couldn't come in because my mom was home, I'd take him to the club house which was usually empty around the time he would come. We'd have sex in the bathroom, then he'd leave.

The more the bills stacked up, the more I looked for him. I ended it when he came by afterwork and was upset at his live-in girlfriend (that I didn't know about) doing some things behind his back while he was locked up. I had walked him to his car when he broke down in tears and threw his phone, shattering it in anger. At that moment, I had had enough of him and didn't want to deal with a man with issues when I had my own.

Late one night, I was all in my feelings of loneliness and did the one thing (of many) that you shouldn't do in those times. Facebook searching for exes because we all know the saying.

Well, I found something, or someone to be exact. I found Nathan. Yes, dear reader, the same Nathan that was mentioned before. To make matters worse, when I sent him a message, he replied instantly. Shake your head but stay with me.

We spent a few minutes messaging before he asked for my number. I obliged. After talking for a few days and finding out that he was living about thirty minutes from my sister, the scheduled trip to her house looked brighter.

I left the kids at my sisters to meet him by myself. We met up at one of the museums to spend the day together and catch up. Knowing this was a bad idea for a ton of reasons, I ignored logic and decided to be led by the butterflies in my stomach. I still had love for him and did not want to pass up the opportunity to spend a day with him. After strolling around the museum, we wanted to go to a more private place to talk. If desperation of intimacy was the fuel, Nathan was the match. We found privacy in a model home.

The sundress I had worn made it easy for us to unite as one satisfying all the needs that had me on Facebook in the first place. While we were searching for a hotel to fully reconnect, the girlfriend he was living with called and wanted to speak to me. Since he lied about his living arrangement, I was more than happy to have a conversation with her. Once the call ended, I got in my car and went back to my sister's leaving him to figure out how to get home.

His calls went unanswered for the remainder of the trip because I was hurt. Back at home, with no job to go to and no suitors to keep me occupied, I called him. His girlfriend kicked him out and he was moving back to his place in Brooklyn. I was back on the Nathan train.

I needed a distraction from the reality I was living, and he was offering that. All I had to do was pick him and his stuff up and take him to Brooklyn. Fine with me. The girls and I got on the road and after dropping them off at my sisters, I went to get him and his things. He said she wasn't home, and he would be waiting outside for me. I picked him up without any drama and went back to my sisters to get the girls. He drove my car to Brooklyn where we stayed with him for two wonderful weeks.

There were a few hiccups during this time like her blowing up my phone every hour until I finally spoke with her. I felt I owed her a conversation. She informed me that she was there when I picked him up. Not at her house but sitting in her car where she wouldn't be seen. It was then I stopped talking to her and blocked her number.

The girls were having a blast being in Brooklyn. Going to the laundromat, riding the trains, hanging out with their cousins and attending a block party. It was the first time they were experiencing New York since we moved several years earlier.

Quick story: As we were passing thrown away furniture, Autumn said, "Oh mommy! They are having a yard sale." I had to inform her, "No sweetie, that is how trash is thrown out. You sit it on the curb for the trashman to pick up." Teagan said, "It stinks here!" to which I explained, "It is the smell of diversity. People from different backgrounds and cultures living in the same place. It's a beautiful smell." She wasn't buying.

During our time there, another hiccup was how my body was acting out. I developed a rash under my breasts that itched and turned my skin scaly and three shades darker. No matter how many showers I took and changed clothes, my deodorant would wear off almost immediately which made for an embarrassing trip to Coney Island with my cousins. It should not have been embarrassing because I was with family. Family I considered myself intimately close with. *Samantha. I'm talking about you!*

It's cool though. I could have told them I was showering often, wearing deodorant and clean clothes. That my body, for some reason beyond my good hygiene was betraying me. I didn't care enough though because I was back home and with the man I loved. We smoked weed, made love, drank and woke up in each other's arms when the girls stayed with family. My body's rebellion did not stop the fun. He was divorced (verified through the papers) and now, no longer with the woman he was living with. He was available for me. When it was time to leave, he gave me a key to come back whenever I wanted.

Back in North Carolina, knowing what I knew about him, I knew he was already looking for the next lady to be with. This did not sit well with me. I was unhappy and desperate for the affection that ended too quickly. I tried to focus on reading the Bible, but it wasn't helping. Mainly because I was just reading and not applying it to my life. Bills were out of control, and every week was a threat to repossess my car.

After those two weeks, we got to see each other once more and made the decision that we didn't want to be apart. His lease was ending at the end of September, and we thought it best that he move in with me in NC. Now, let me say that I knew this was bullshit because you have more than a week or two notice that your lease is expiring. But I didn't care. I was selfish and only thinking of me and my needs. I didn't care that my mother wasn't supportive. He adored my girls, and I knew he would never bring them harm. My sanity and depression needed his company.

By the end of November, I was hiding a pregnancy that I did not want. He was comfortable but reluctant with my decision to terminate and took me to the clinic. He understood how I couldn't see myself ever being able to love a baby enough to have it grow just for it to die on me. Been there and I couldn't go back.

Emotionally, I was unattached to the thought of a pregnancy. Physically, it didn't take long for my stomach to swell, which I blamed on all the eating over Thanksgiving. Mentally, I was suffering from a clear reminder of only holding my babies in death. The 3-tier nightmare started increasing in frequency. This fetus had to go. *And yes. I was still having the dream, and it still included Kamar. I would call him or his dad to make sure he was alive.*

I declined being put to sleep. I wanted to feel all the pain and pressure of this termination as a punishment to myself. What's strange is that with this being the second pregnancy after the twins passed, this one made me hurt differently. Maybe because with Chase, there was history and discussion of keeping it. With this one, keeping it wasn't an option, yet I grieved just as hard. Mainly for the loss of my boys.

Let me explain something. It is now three years since my boys passed away. I was still unable to walk down any baby aisle or even look in that direction. If there was a person in the aisle with a baby, I left and went to another aisle until they left so I could get what I needed. Whenever I saw twins, I had a panic attack. At church, there were twins being dedicated and I had to leave the sanctuary because of a very nasty panic attack.

I could not participate in certain types of conversations. Baby showers were completely out of the question as was holding a baby. I once held Carlos's newborn and not even a minute went by before I had to hand her back because of the tightness in my chest which was always how my panic attacks started.

I was still grieving. I didn't *and still don't* like to be told Happy Mother's Day except by my kids because it reminds me that my motherhood is incomplete. Missing two. So, no. The thought of having a baby was not an option.

On a clear, warm winters night in December, I was out on the balcony starring at the stars smoking and talking to God like I normally did. *God and I had our deepest one-way conversations out on the balcony while I smoked.* I told Him how sorry I was that I could not keep the blessing He had given to us. That I couldn't face the pain of pregnancy for it to end with a dead baby in my arms. I smoked, cried, and poured my heart out looking towards the heavens to make sure He heard my remorse, even if all the talking was being done silently. I said I was sorry and asked for forgiveness for the hundredth time and I was reminded that I had been forgiven. After all, it is us that keeps going back to our sins.

Hebrews 8:12 For I will be merciful to their unrighteousness, and their sins and their lawless deeds I will remember no more. I wish I could be like God in that manner. Forget my sins. But, since I'm human and can't forget, the next best thing I can do is forgive myself. *And I have.*

That night I cried myself to sleep for all the hurt I caused God with every termination I had. I vowed to never have another abortion. Even now, I commend every female that choose to have their baby despite their age or circumstance. *Don't get me wrong, I am still pro-choice.*

I know whether the decision to have a baby or not is personal and not always easy to make. My view is just a little different now that I look at it as God's loss and how it may hurt Him. My wish would be for no one to ever have to experience that devastation. Not even God.

The relationship between Nathan and I was not affected by this abortion. He was working and helping as he could with the household expenses. It wasn't until I started working in and he became unemployed that we started having problems.

While I was at work, he started cheating. I found this out by taking his phone when I heard him say "I love you also and I'll see you soon." The woman on the other end told me they have been talking back and forth, and he was going to come and spend time with her next week. The week he told me he was heading back to NY to see his kids. I put her on speaker and told them both that they didn't need to wait until next week. He would be on his way that night. "I know it's April Fool's Day, but I am not joking. Nathan, pack your shit and get out."

After a tearful goodbye between him and my girls, he gathered his things and left in a cab that night. I wasn't upset. After all, it was just karma coming back to me.

At the Altar

As a young girl growing up in the church, there were several Bible stories that left me in awe and blew my mind.

The parting of the Red Sea, and the plagues that preceded it. Jesus calming the stormy sea was more impressive than Peter walking on water, in my opinion. Did you know that baby replacement is nothing new? It's in the Old Testament. Except she was down for cutting the baby in half. What about the man who sent his daughter to get raped by a mob of men who wanted to rape his male houseguest?

The one that always tugged at me, the woman with the issue of blood.

The retelling of the woman with the issue of blood can be found in several scriptures in the New Testament. Matthew 9: 20-22, Mark 5: 25-34, and Luke 8: 43-48. This woman spent twelve years on her menstrual. This caused her to be an outcast among her family and community. What captured me about her, even at a young age, was her faith. Faith that caused her to believe that if she could just touch Jesus, she would be healed.

I would close my eyes whenever I thought of her and prayed for Jesus to let me just touch the hem of his garment like this bold woman. He could remove all my sadness with just one touch. An image of a hem trailing at his feet on a dusty road would be my vision and touching it. Imagine how many hands were already touching his garment? Hands of people that I'm sure had their own ailments. What faith this woman exhibited that He felt HER touch? This had me looking up to her even in my adult years, often wondering if I could ever trust in Jesus enough to humble myself to crawl behind him and touch his garment.

I was about to find out.

I don't remember what Sunday in July it was when I first heard a little whisper tell me to *"crawl to the altar."* I do know it was after the Pastor finished preaching and I was crying as he led everyone into worship. Even in 2011, I was still crying a lot. *And avoiding all the things I told you about in the last chapter.*

My first thought was "hell no." It was a packed church, and I sat in the back. That crawl would not be a two-step type of crawl as if I sat in the front pew. I looked towards the altar wondering what I would look like crawling. Seeing the camera stand I would have to pass. Looking at all the pews I would have to pass. We are not a mega church, but we are not a small church either.

The next Sunday, after Pastor preached, I heard *"crawl to the altar, your healing is waiting at the altar."* Why? What healing did I need? I wasn't sick. That day after church, having a cigarette on the balcony, I spoke to God concerning the instruction. I didn't get any feedback and dismissed the thought. I started thinking that maybe I had lung cancer and didn't know it. I still smoked every day several times a day.

Another Sunday came and went. I played with the idea of doing it but when I thought about it, it didn't feel genuine. Maybe because I thought about it without having instructions to do it. Out of my mind it went. Then, the voice came again as Pastor was finishing his sermon and many people were shouting. The sanctuary was loud with the voices of praise and music. Yet, I heard the whisper. *"There is a healing waiting for you. To receive it, you must crawl to the altar."* Can't I walk I asked in my head. *"No. You must crawl and not worry what others may think. This is only for you, and I won't tell you again."* Well, the thought of missing out on an unknown healing was enough to make my legs move.

I was wearing a brown skirt with flowers on the bottom with a beige Aeropostale shirt and dark brown sandals with a 4-inch heel from Nine West. The skirt came a little past my knees. This isn't important, just showing how much I remember from that day like it was yesterday. I was still near the back but in the middle of the row. I made my way to the end of the pew and took a step out. *"I will meet you at the altar. Crawl."*

I did. Immediately, I fell to my knees and began to crawl. Once that first crawl started, tears came flooding out of my eyes and I wasn't aware of anyone in that church. As I reached the altar, the words "I killed my babies" came out of my mouth a few times. I believed those words. Chase blamed me because I was their mother and should have kept them alive. I blamed myself because in the back of my mind was always family history, and my lack of faith with Jaden. I blamed myself for the two cigarettes I smoked while pregnant. Their death was on my hands.

I said those words again, "I killed my babies". I was still on my knees when these words were proclaimed from my mouth. I remember falling with my face in my hands touching the floor while on my knees. While I was in this position, darkness rushed in and enveloped me. I have been in darkness before, however, this time it was different. The atmosphere was thick. I could see nothing. It was darkness darker than just closing your eyes in a dark room. It was quiet. No sound at all. And although it was heavy darkness, it didn't feel suffocating, and I wasn't scared. Nor did I feel alone.

There was something with me that comforted me. Stood me up and surrounded me. It gave me peace. I don't know if it was Christ Himself or an angel. Either way, with the darkness on all sides, there was the warm embrace of a Spirit. I didn't feel a need to run away. It felt good to be in the warmness. It was in this warmth that I felt my heart mending. The same way I felt it breaking when told of Khalil's death. There I was, standing in this space with a presence that I knew was with me. After feeling as if my heart was whole, the atmosphere transitioned. Darkness no longer occupied it. It now looked like the sky does at sunset. Orange and blue hues moving in slow motion.

Then it was bright again.

The first thing I noticed was that I was not standing, but still on my knees with my face in my hands. I heard the Pastor talking. The music was no longer loud with worship and praise, but soft and low. I brought my head up and said with a smile "I didn't kill my babies" and I believed it. I locked eyes with the Pastor who was still speaking softly and said it again. "I didn't kill my babies." There was no immediate yes you did. No reasons why the statement wasn't true. I said it again just to be sure. Again, there were no opposing voices.

As I stood up, the next thing I noticed was an odor coming from me. My deodorant had said bye while I was away from me. I then assessed my surroundings all with a smile on my face. My mother and other ministers and deacons started walking back to their seats from surrounding me.

As I walked past all the pews stinking, I didn't even care. My soul was rejoicing. Doing flips because I knew without a shadow of a doubt that I did not kill Khalil and Jaden. I was smiling wide, not even covering my face. Just cheesing repeating these words in my head. I did not kill my babies. By the time I got to my seat, Pastor started giving the benediction. It made me wonder how much time had passed.

In the car, I was giddy and on a natural high. I asked my mother if she knew what happened because I was not there in spirit. I heard nothing at all. She only said that Pastor was praying over me, and several people had their hands on me praying. They covered me and prayed. *I felt none of them nor did I hear them.*

I was excited about the fact that I could now declare that I did not kill Khalil, and I did not kill Jaden! I wanted to tell everyone. I called my sister, my girlfriends Asha and Nicole telling them all with joy from deep within that I experienced a healing I didn't know I needed.

I didn't know how much weight I was holding on to from thinking and believing I killed my boys. That my fears destroyed their ability to live. Those thoughts that held me bound were released. I imagine the release of my deodorant left with the bondage of those thoughts. Kamar was with us since it was the summertime, and I cooked a big celebratory meal and dessert.

I experienced a healing that only came to me from obedience to the Spirit telling me to crawl to the altar. I don't beat myself up for not listening the first time nor the second time. To me, it is my assurance that despite my smoking. Despite my fornication. Despite the abortions. God loved me enough to want to set me free!

That healing affected my life on so many levels. Levels that I didn't realize until months later. So many chains of bondage were released in that healing. Chains I didn't even realize were connected. Like it took weeks for me to notice that I no longer had the 3-tiered nightmare.

The manipulation that Chase had over me was gone because he could no longer hold guilt of their deaths over me. Not until writing this chapter, did I realize that I have not had any phantom sex either. Nor has the darkness ever visited me again.

Healing is not just from sickness, disease, or addiction. Healing can be from thoughts or beliefs that you have about yourself that keep you in a mental and emotional prison.

I was healed in August of 2011, five years to the month they originally due. Even after ignoring what I know with every fiber of my being was Jesus telling me what I needed to do. I thank God for not letting my first no, be my last no. I thank God for second chance after second chance.

I did not kill Khalil.

I did not kill Jaden.

No one will EVER be able to convince me otherwise.

What thoughts are holding you back from peace and joy? What does God want to heal you from? What are you willing to do to find out? It may not be crawling to an altar. It may be something as simple as just talking with God. I pray He leads you on a path of discovery. I want everyone to experience God's healing in their life.

I was so elated that I wanted to see something. The next week I purposely went to Babies R Us. The moment I walked in, my chest started tightening up and I started crying. I took a couple of deep breaths and continued on. A store clerk asked if I was okay and I replied that I was. And I really was. Although my chest got tight, it didn't turn into a panic attack. I walked that whole store and by the time I left I was no longer crying.

This healing did not stop me from smoking, fornicating, drinking, or having depression and suicidal ideation. There were times that I would get mad at God for not giving me an instant healing from these things, especially when I would beat myself up for them. I would then remember it is a process and sometimes He works on one thing at a time. You may need healing in one area to prepare you for another. I thank God for starting the process on me. My soul is better for it. And just knowing that Jesus cares for a sinner like me makes me shout HALLELUJAH!!!! Even a sinner can hear the voice of God.

Oh! Mighty God. I pray that every reader of this book is touched by You in a way that cannot be denied. That You heal whatever it is in their life that can only be done by You. Be it a thought or illness. May they experience a hem of Your garment faith healing Jesus, so they know that in THAT instant, You, have healed them. And whatever faith You have them step out on can only be traced back to You. Sending a Thank you ahead of the healing. In the precious and mighty name of Jesus. Amen.

BOOK FOUR

Hidden Behind Destiny

Proverbs 18:21 Death and life are in the power of the tongue, and those who love it will eat it's fruit.

You must be careful what you put out in the atmosphere. Sometimes you verbalize things that you want to happen. For instance, speaking life into a job you want or declaring that a house is yours. The thing with verbalizing what you want is that the Earth is also the devil's arena. If you don't believe me, turn in your Bible to the first book of Job, the first chapter verses 6 and 7.

Now there was a day when the sons of God came to present themselves before the Lord, and Satan also came among them. And the Lord said to Satan, "From where do you come?" So Satan answered the Lord and said, "From going to and fro on the earth, and from walking back and forth on it."

The devil hears everything you speak. And although he is not God, able to give you the desires of heart, when you speak those desires, he can deliver. When he does, you would think that it was God's doing. I found this out firsthand when I became fixated on no longer being by myself but in a relationship. Talking to my friend Asha about how I was tired of not having a man in my life to potentially settle down with after Nathan and I didn't work out yet again. Chatting with co-workers about my desire to be in a relationship. Friends. Family. Whoever would listen.

One day at lunch, I was talking about my loneliness and how I did miss Nathan. He was my familiar space. It must have got on their nerves because they suggested that I needed night on the town. I couldn't agree more.

We decided to go to the bar, eat and then go to the club. At the first place we went to, one of the ladies got out to go see how crowded it was. She came back and determined it was too empty for me to find a man. Out of the five of us, I was the only single one. They wanted me to find someone, and it wasn't going to happen in an empty bar. We then went to another spot, but it was closed. We headed to the club, but the line was wrapped around the block, no parking and we did not feel like standing in a line. Back to the first bar we went.

We created our own fun space, and the live band created the club atmosphere. We drank, danced and talked. In all our fun, I needed to use the restroom. I passed a couple on the way and secretly wished that was me. On the way back, passing the same couple, the gentleman caught my eye. He was older, but I felt that I knew him from somewhere. Back at the table, I kept staring because there was something about him.

Going through my mental photograph book, I knew he couldn't be someone from NC. I didn't know many men here. Then he smiled a big smile, and I recognized him. It was Nathan. *Haha just joking. It was Derrick.*

I walked over to them, spoke to the lady first by asking if it was alright to speak to her companion letting her know I went to Junior High School with him. He was focused on making his shot that he didn't even notice I approached her. She gave her permission, not that I was looking for it but was trying to be respectful. I approached him and asked.

"Are you Derrick?"
"Yeah and who are you?"
"You may not remember me but I'm LaChelle from Bushwick. We went to school together." He is thinking.
"Oh my God! LaChelle from Bushwick. Fuck yeah, I remember you."
(To his girlfriend) "Yo! We went to Junior High School together. LaChelle from Bushwick. She gave me her virginity."

(Awkward laughter) "Yeah I did." (To his girlfriend) "We were young and stupid." (Back to Derrick) "How have you been?" (To his girlfriend) "I need a smoke. Want one?" (she replied no then back to me) "Come talk to me and catch up while I have a smoke." (in a loud animated voice) "LaChelle from fucking Bushwick oh shit. Who are you here with."
"My friends over there."

On the way out, I introduced him to my friends. As we were walking out, I heard him say something, but I didn't catch it. I needed my heart and pulse to calm the fuck down.

Outside he offered me a cigarette and there went several months being smoke free out the window. I needed that cigarette though. I needed it badly. Here I was, standing in front of the guy I once loved with all my teenage heart and who I found worthy of giving my virginity to. There was no way I was going to pass this meeting up.

About two cigarettes into our conversation, his girlfriend comes out telling him to pay the tab she is leaving. He tells her not to leave and proceeds to toss out his cigarette and tell me he must go because they came together. But first he asked me if I drove there. I told him no, and he went in to handle their tab. I remained outside finishing the cigarette and gathering my thoughts. We exchanged numbers and he left.

"It's about time you came back in. His girlfriend kept looking towards the door and we felt bad for her. Plus, when you guys were going out I asked what about his girl and his reply was, "That bitch will be ok." I said nothing. I went to sit quietly on a stool with my drink. "Now you a smoker again?" I said nothing. A group of guys came in and took the table next to us. They tried to hook me up with one of them, but I wasn't feeling it. I watched my girls have a good time laughing and partying with these guys as they brought us a round of drinks.

Fast forward a few weeks of phone conversations. Him and his girlfriend had broken up leaving us free to meet up. My mom was going away for a week, and I decided to have him over. He didn't have a car and was currently a weekly paying resident at a hotel.

I took my daughters with me to pick him up since they weren't old enough to stay home by themselves. When we got back to my place, I put them to bed while he took my car to go get some beer. He came back with a six pack of Coronas. We went out on the balcony to drink, smoke and conversate. On the balcony, he wanted to tell me something important face-to-face.

He was attending anger management classes because he caught his girlfriend cheating and went ballistic. Destroyed her television and slapped her. Then he states that at first, he didn't want to go out but she kept insisting. How happy he was that he gave in, or we never would have met. I told him how I ended up at that bar, and he said our paths were destined to meet. After my girls had been asleep for a few hours, we ended up having sex which was uneventful. Kind of like losing my virginity to him all over again.

In the following weeks, there were a lot of things about Derrick I choose to ignore. Things like how he was showing me how selfish he was. The nights I spent at the hotel with him; I would always be late for work because he would cancel his ride and have me to take him to work. I had to be at work at eight and so did he, but he didn't like getting there early. He didn't like it when I dropped him off by 7:30 a.m. so I could make it to my place of employment on time. He'd complain it was too cold to wait outside. No matter how much I rushed him, we never seemed to leave the hotel until 7:30/7:45 a.m. He would be on time, and I would get to work by 8:30 a.m. or after. But I choose to ignore it because I was finally in a relationship again.

Late November or early in December, we found out I was knocked up. It still came to me as a shock. Yes, we were having unprotected sex, but after that last abortion, I thought God understood that I never wanted another baby. I cried because I knew I had to have it but didn't want to. When I told Derrick, he was fine and suggested we get married. We both had kids out of wedlock (he had two) and he didn't want that for this one.

When I told my mother, I asked her if it would be ok for him to move in. She stated that if he would be moving in as a husband and not a boyfriend, she would be ok with that. She also asked me if I was seeking God to find out if he was the one for me. I wasn't but soon would be.

We decided to get married at the courthouse two weeks after finding out we were expecting. I wasn't in love with him but did love him. I had reservations about him due to the issue of his drinking that I didn't care for and the amount of weed he smoked. These complaints took a backseat to the fact that I was having sex again. Not on the level of Nathan or Chase and I had to be ok with that. There were times he told me no that he just wanted to hold me and sleep. Those nights I rolled my eyes, snuggled next to him and tired but to no avail. We just slept.

Only one friend from work attended my wedding. I confided to her how I felt while waiting for the Judge to call us in. Disappointment that this was not the wedding I had planned for myself. Disappointment that he was not Nathan. However, selfish reasons made me plant me feet and proceed to become his wife.

We got married for our own selfish reasons and the baby was the cover. Derrick married me to get out of living in a hotel and have access to a car. I got married so I could have sex under the authority of marriage without guilt of not going by the word of God. That sex only comes after marriage. This baby created the opportunity for both of us. And for us, when asked, our chance meeting became our answer. Destiny brought us together. Anyone we told the story to would agree.

For our honeymoon, he surprised me with a weekend stay in the mountains. We spent that first night high and drunk. Here is where I will explain to you why I was smoking weed & cigarettes and drinking. One, it was the fun Derrick bought for both of us. Two, I at first declined but then he started complaining he didn't want to be the only one celebrating. That a little of the natural stuff and some alcohol wouldn't do the baby any damage. Three, when I first found out I was pregnant, I stopped smoking. This was the first weekend I had indulged.

Looking back, I believe we both knew deep down we didn't want a baby. Yes. I know I said that an abortion wasn't an option, and it wasn't. That doesn't mean I had to be over the moon thrilled that I got myself in the situation. It just meant I had to suck it up and mentally prepare to carry a baby and hopefully love it after it was born.

After spending the Christmas holiday with my sister and her family, where Derrick did not get me a gift. Then going to visit my son before heading to New York to re-meet his family, we came back home to get ready for our first pre-natal visit. I was scared going to the doctor's office. Derrick couldn't make it because of work and might not make it in time, but he was going to try. I was nervous and spent the time in the waiting room debating if I wanted to see the sonogram or not. *Should I wait to love it until after 24 weeks? Will they force me to hear the heartbeat? Does it have one this early?* I couldn't remember.

When the doctor first did the ultrasound and stepped out of the room and came back with someone else, I knew that something was wrong. She then turned to me and told me that there wasn't a heartbeat, and it probably stopped a week or so ago. She said that since it hadn't dislodged itself from my body, I could continue carrying until it did, or have it surgically removed. The doctor then left me alone with my tears until Derrick arrived.

Asking God if the honeymoon night of weed and alcohol stopped its heart. Not able to pinpoint the exact timeframe left me with more questions than answers. Questioning God if He took away this blessing because He knew what was down the road. Was He correcting a mistake? Yes, yes, yes. I know what you may be thinking. God doesn't make mistakes. Let the church stand and turn to I Samuel 15: 10 – 11

Now the word of the Lord came to Samuel, saying "I greatly regret that I have set up Saul as king, for he has turned back from following Me, and has not performed My commandments." And it grieved Samuel, and he cried out to the Lord all night.

For argument's sake, maybe God removed the fetus not because He made a mistake but simply regretted giving me the blessing and took it back. Either way, the fetus was no more. As I laid in the doctors' office and cried, I must be honest with you. Those tears were not for this pregnancy but for the renewed feeling of loss for my boys.

The next week, Derrick and I went to the hospital to have it removed. He was very husband like for the next two weeks. Catering to my emotional and physical needs. Nothing sexual, just holding me until I slept. I learned my lesson from after having Teagan that refraining from sex during the time the doctor gives is for health reasons. Let's just say Chase and I wanted to have sex so bad that I ended up in the hospital with doctors using me as a lesson and curious residents just wanting to see. It cost me three weeks of pain and permanent hemorrhoids.

It was during this time; I started seeking God regarding him like my mom had asked if I was doing. The realization that I was now in a marriage without any reason to show for it, made me work harder on falling in love. I didn't want to get out of the marriage because I did love him. But I also knew, even if I didn't share it with my friends or family, why I needed this marriage to work.

Classes? What Classes?

After the follow-up doctor visit, the reality of our situation came into complete focus. We married out of convenience. Even though we never uttered it to each other, we didn't have to. We were not in love. I am not sure Derrick even loved me a little bit. Sure, he acted as if he was happy to have a wife, but I don't believe there was love behind it. He did little big things.

Once we were married, he would take my car most days dropping me off at work since I didn't mind being early. Sometimes, he would pick me up late because he went to smoke with co-workers after work leaving me in the office at times until 6-7 p.m. I got off at five.

One time when I had my car and went to pick him up, he had me waiting in the parking lot for over an hour while he and his co-workers got high. The last time I got high was the night we came home from the hospital. I wasn't into weed the way he was. Times when the tire pressure would be low, he'd tell me he couldn't be late for work and would continue driving to his job leaving me to go to the gas station and fill the tires up with air on my way to work. I was doing that when I was single, why did I have to do it with a husband? There was one time when the tank needing filling. I had to do it while he sat in the passenger seat because he didn't want to get out in the cold. I never allowed that to happen again.

It was those little big things that showed me he wasn't going to try and make this marriage work. I did try because I didn't want to give up, well, you know what I didn't want to give up. Too bad even that was slowly decreasing. One evening, I picked him up from work with my panties in my pocketbook. Thinking that would turn him on. I was wrong. He called me a hoe, turned the music up and lit a cigarette. I was confused. I simply replied that he didn't say that before and not to call me out my name.

The name-calling increased after trying twice to co-sign with him to purchase a vehicle and being denied both times. When I suggested he stop trying to get a new car and look for one being sold by an owner, he told me I needed to get my credit up. I thought that maybe he should get his credit up and he wouldn't need a co-signer. I looked at it as God blocking me from becoming financially bound to someone he did not send. Remember, I started praying for God to show me if this was the person for me. It was a little late to be asking when I knew the answer all along.

No. I choose this path without direction from God. Ignoring the signs. I gladly wore blinders, ignored the alarms, and disregarded Maya Angelou's words. *When people show you who they are, believe them.* I didn't. Instead, I started praying for God to change who he was.

While shopping in Walmart, a photo from a group chat my co-workers and I were in came through my phone. I replied to the text. As we were standing in line, I was still texting.

"Derrick, look at this photo." I said laughing.
"No. Stay in line I forgot to get cheese."

By time he came back, we had reached the register. Since he was making all the purchases, it allowed me time to continue texting. When we got in the car, he turned to me and accused me of texting the dude in the next aisle. What?

"I saw you texting him when I came back with the cheese."
"What dude? What are you talking about? You knew I was chatting with my friends." Then more back and forth arguing.
"Why were you so busy minding the business of another man in another aisle anyway when I didn't even notice him?"

"You are nothing but a dirty little bitch. I married a fucking dirty whore. Fucking slut."

I couldn't say anything else. I was too busy wondering why he was minding the business of another man in another aisle when I didn't even notice him. When we got home and started putting the groceries away, he stated that I needed to stop being their friend because they don't like him.

"Your friend called me a bitch and cursed me out and you just sat there letting her talk to your husband any kind of way."
"And what did you say to her?"
"I called her a bitch like she is and hung up on her."
"Is that all that happened?"
"You don't need to be friends with them if they are going to be disrespectful to me. You need to stop being their friend before you allow them to brainwash you against me."
"You know? You are right. They don't like you."

Let me tell you how she came to call him out his name on the phone.

This event transpired a few weeks after the miscarriage and before he first started with the name-calling. We went out for a night of dancing to get my mind off things. He was picking me up from the club enabling me to drink as much as I wanted because he promised to be my designated driver. After a few hours, I decided that I was ready to go home. When he came into the club to pick me up, he was high. It was all on his face. One look at him and you knew he was high and drunk. That upset me because he said he wouldn't drink or smoke. I was the only one allowed that night to embellish.

In the club, he started getting loud with me and pulling me forcibly back onto the dance floor. I was upset with him and started sobering up quickly because of the way he was acting. Plus, I wasn't drunk, just tipsy or feeling nice you might say.

It got worse when I refused to dance with him and just wanted to go home. My friends started telling him to chill and that is when he accused me in a very loud voice of "fucking the dudes in the club." This really ticked my friends off because they knew I was just out for a good time and wasn't dancing with anyone but them or by myself. I finally had enough and said goodnight to them and walked out of the club with Derrick shouting behind me over the music.

"Don't you want to tell the guys you fucked you leaving?"

Once outside, I told Derrick I would drive because by now, I was completely sober. He refused to give up the keys and proceeded towards the car. Once in the car, he reached over to feel between my legs. He speculated that my panties were wet because I, "Just finished fucking a dude or dudes like the slut that you are." He did not want to listen as I explained that it was sweat. The same sweat that made the style in my hair drop. The same sweat that made my dress damp. It was only sweat. He called me names and threw accusations for the entire ride home.

When we pulled up to the apartment, I wanted my keys. Keys he refused to give up even after telling him I needed to go upstairs and use the bathroom. He didn't budge and did not park. He sat in front of our building telling me to get out the car, so he could go back out. I was not letting him take my car anywhere else that night. I really had to pee, so I opened the door and prayed he wouldn't pull off as I preceded to use the bathroom with my ass hanging.

As I got tired of hearing his rant about me having sex with random guys in the club, I called my friend and put her on speakerphone. I asked her if I had sex tonight and she said no and cursed him out. He snatched the phone, called her a bitch and hung up. He then pulled off. I asked him where we were going and if he could slow down. It was after 2 am and the streets were empty and quiet. He said since I liked living dangerously, he could kill us both tonight. I looked over at the speedometer and noticed he was going over 90 on a stretch of road that was 35 mph. I prayed hard for a policeman to pull us over.

After a few of my requests for him to slow down went ignored, I yelled that he was a fucking paranoid asshole. This comment made him pull over and told me to say it again and see if he doesn't blacken both my eyes. I knew he meant what he threatened because it was in his face and the balled-up fist that was waiting.

Quickly, I thought about my options and settled on fighting in the car this night if that is what it would come down to. I thought it would be best if with this first threat of physical violence, I didn't back down. He needed to know he wouldn't be able to control me. With fear and quiet confidence that I was not feeling *I was terrified of getting punched in the face*, I looked him in his eyes and said very slowing emphasizing each word, "You are a fucking paranoid asshole."

"You must really want me to fucking punch you?" He lightly slaps me. "Say that shit again and I will bloody your mouth." "I already said it, and you heard me clearly. I don't need to say it again." This was said with a calm I was not feeling. It's like I was in my head running around trying to put out fires that were all over the place with an empty bucket.

Next thing I know, he is pulling off and heading back home without another word. He parked, and we went inside to a sleeping house. He opened the balcony door and threw my keys over and told me, "Go get your fucking keys bitch." I ignored him and went into the bathroom to shower then went to bed. The next morning, the keys were on the counter where they belonged.

My prayers to God intensified. They became a request for a change in Derrick, so our marriage would work. I wasn't ready to give up on him or us. By now, he had started denying me sex. Saying only whores wanted to have sex all the time. This confused me because he was my husband and from past relationships, no one ever denied me sex. It also caused me to wonder if he was the one cheating. I figured he was projecting his actions onto me. I started praying even harder.

Lord, I come to you requesting that you change Derrick. Take his anger and hostility away and open his heart to love. Help me to become the wife that he needs. I know you can make this change in an instant because you do not work in time. Lord, I am starting to think that our meeting was not orchestrated by you. But now that I am in it, I am asking for your help. If this marriage is not in your will, please make this known. Amen.

One Day I'll Get It Right

To try and rekindle something that was never there, I suggested we go out. He agreed, and we went out on a date. We went to a spot in our neighborhood and had a good time. That was until he got more beer in him than was necessary. By the time we were on our third game, the bartender kicked us out for his loud profanity. As I was driving us home, he started accusing me again of cheating.

"I know you had someone over the house fucking in my bed the other day. You thought I wouldn't notice."
"What are you talking about now?"
"You know what I'm talking about. Don't play that stupid hoe shit with me now that you got caught."
"Got caught doing what? I don't know what you are talking about." I said with exasperation.
"Last Saturday, when I left for work in the morning and came back, there was another pillow on the bed and a damp washcloth on the nightstand."
"Really Derrick? I woke up with a migraine and my feet were swollen so I had the cloth over my head and used the pillow to elevate my feet."
"No. You are a lying whore who got caught."
"And you are a paranoid alcoholic who needs to pay more attention in your anger management classes and now your nonsense made me miss my turn."
"I made you miss the turn? I made you miss the turn? Turn this bitch."

He then proceeds to move the gear shift between park, reverse and drive all while I was driving. I pushed his hand away and pulled into a vacant lot.

In the lot, I put the car in park and turned off the ignition for the car to rest after his antics. He sees this as an opportunity to yank the keys out and throw them. As I get out to retrieve them, he is following close behind and pushes me. I turn around and push him back then head for the keys and pick them up. When I rise from bending, he pushes me again, all the while accusing me of cheating. We are shouting at each other interrupting the quiet night. He slaps me hard. I return the jester and now we are fighting. He heads to the car and started kicking it. Then pulls out his knife and threatens to slash the tires.

"You know only jealous bitches slash tires. Are you a jealous bitch Derrick?"
"Keep talking out the side of your mouth and see if I don't slash them."
"Yes, because that would be the smart thing to do. Why would you slash my tires when we both have jobs to go to? How are we going to get to work if we have a car with no tires? How are we going to get home? Fucking idiot."

Just as he is starting to rush at me, two cop cars pull up into the parking lot. They get out and advise that they had several calls from the neighboring houses of a couple fighting. I let them know that my husband has had too much to drink and is accusing me of cheating. Each of them takes our id and separates us one per officer. After assuring them that nothing is wrong and that we will go home quietly, the officer talking to me reminds me that if I am ever in a position where my safety is compromised, I should call them. Derrick's officer wants to know how he got the scratches on his arm and face and if he wanted to press any charges. Since he didn't, they let us go after assessing the minor damage of dents to the car. They advise us to go home and if they have to come back, one of us or both of us will be leaving with them.

We get back into the car with me behind the wheel, not saying anything to each other. As I drive past our complex, Derrick wants to know where we are going. "I'm driving you to your friend's house. You need to go somewhere and calm the fuck down." He yells at me, "turn around and drive home. I'm not going anywhere." I don't. He tells me again and I ignore him praying he doesn't mess with the gears again. I have one hand on the wheel and the other resting on the gear shift just in case. He grabs the wheel and turns it towards him causing us to jump the curb barely missing the lamp post. "Now take us the fuck home!" I restart the car, turn around and head home.

The next day, my arm is tender with bruises and Derrick is nursing multiple scratches, we get up and attend church for the girls' baptism. Carlos and his kids meet us at the church to come back to the house for dinner. During the service, Derrick was so stone-faced that when I looked at him, I felt like I was sitting next to a demon because his pupils had turned black. The feeling was so strong that I prayed right then for the demonic forces to leave his body. Back at the house, Carlos brought over some beer and commented that Derrick seemed quite and asked if everything was ok.

"Sure, we just had a little fight last night broken up by the police. When we left to head home, he took the car off the road because I wanted to take him to his friends to cool off. Nothing major."

"Damn. You'll acting so normal, you should have told me not to bring any beer. I'll take it back home with me."

That Monday, I left work early to go down to the precinct, and then the courthouse to file for a temporary restraining order. He was served that evening.

Pastors always preach about staying together and working things out with your spouse when things get tough. To not call it quits when the fire gets too hot. I would listen screaming for them to mention the disclaimer. Mention that if your husband is abusive, you need to leave. Very rarely did this disclaimer get put in the sermons. This was another reason why I was praying for God to change his behavior. I felt that to leave would be quitting on my marriage. But anyone who gets a restraining order and then agrees to counseling all in the first three months shouldn't put in any more work.

Asha bet that we wouldn't make it to a year. My co-workers were betting on it being over before we hit six months. I could not disagree, but I was praying. Two days after he was served, he called, and we agreed to meet in person and talk.

Our meeting happened at one of the hotels in the area. Once we started speaking, he acknowledged that he had issues and had to bring this up in his class where they helped him see he was wrong for letting things get out of control. He offered to go to counseling together. We had great sex, and he won me back. At the next court appearance, I dropped the restraining order. The judge read back to me my complaint when I said I would drop it. After she read it, she informed me that she would allow me to drop it without prejudice, meaning I could refile it if needed. Before leaving her courtroom, she advised, "A man who had already gotten physical, taken a car off the road, and threatened your life and theirs would not just stop and change."

"I understand your Honor."
"Hopefully, I won't see you back or read about you. Take care and love your children more if you can't love yourself."
"Thank you, your Honor."

When my co-workers found out that I wanted to work on my marriage, the situation was taken to social media where I was put on blast without the use of my name. I was also kicked out of the group chat and shunned at work by all except the one that helped me get ready for my wedding. What I thought was a solid friendship was over. To this day, I miss them. Haven't connected with another group of ladies since. They couldn't understand my logic to stay. I didn't see myself in an abusive marriage. He never gave me black eyes, busted my lip or broke any bones and I needed no hospital visit. For these reasons, I had a hard time calling it what it was. Domestic abuse.

I figured if I could get him to channel the anger into sex play, then maybe we would be ok. Being with Chase made me explore that side of dominating sex and I found I enjoyed it. If I could get him to see that choking me during sex was more pleasurable for the both of us, maybe we would have a chance.

However, when I brought this alternative up in therapy, he stayed quiet. In the car, he said, "You are a sick mental cunt." That was the only therapy session we attended. Later during the ride when he became talkative again, we started discussing our marriage. As the discussion got heated, he started to drive faster than the speed limit. About 30 miles over the posted 70. After my pleas for him to slow down went unanswered and fueled him more. I decided to keep my mouth shut, prayed and smoked a cigarette.

He moved back in and for a short while, things were nice. We went out more with and without my daughters. He never attended church with me again and that was fine by me. The vibe of him sitting next to me at the baptismal was one that I did not want to repeat. We were having sex right after work and he even played with me in the car without calling me any derogatory names.

I encouraged him to investigate starting his own business. He was very talented, and I thought his talent was being wasted and taken for granted on his job. His retort would be that it was the best place to work. His boss was not only a friend but sometimes supplied the beer and weed for after work. I would tell him that wasn't a reason to continue working and not try his hand at his own business. But, if you have ever watched a Lifetime movie, you know this truce didn't last. Before I knew it, the name-calling was back, and the denial of sex was back. In came the fighting and praying even harder.

There was nothing in particular that would set him off. When he was drinking and getting high, which was every day, anything would make him upset with me. On this day, it was the fact that I said no to trying to aid him again in getting a vehicle. He had found one being sold by an owner for $1,700.00 and wanted me to give him 1K of that. The reason I gave was that he wasn't helping with the rent or bills like he was supposed to so why would I fork that money over? We argued and fought. I ducked one of his punches and he put a hole in our closet door instead. He pushed the screen out the window and threated to toss my phone out of it. When I went out on the balcony to get away and have a smoke, he followed me. Tried to pick me up to toss me over. I came inside and called 911.

"911 is this an emergency?"
"Yes, this is (name) at (address) and I ordered a pizza and was wondering when it would get here."
"Mam' this is 911, do you have an emergency."
"Yes, I'm at (address) and it's been over an hour for the delivery."
"Is he in the room with you?"
"Large pepperoni and sausage."
"Does he have a weapon?"
"No but how long will it be?"
"I'm dispatching a car to your address now. Are you able to stay on the line?"
"I don't know, we are really hungry." Derrick has now come in from the balcony cursing and calling me names. My mom comes out of her bedroom telling us to stop the fighting, we woke her up and are going to wake up the girls.
"Can you throw in some breadsticks?"
"You calling the cops on me bitch?'
"I need to go thank you."

It was after one am by the time the cops escorted Derrick out of the apartment. I went to bed crying listening to *I Won't Give Up* by Jason Mraz on repeat. I didn't want to give up, but I knew this was not God's plan. I realized that. The realization that God did not bring us together freed me but also devastated me. All the love I tried to give. All the encouragement that was always one sided. I was always pouring positivity into his talent, yet he never poured anything into me.

A little after four am, he called me asking if I could give him a ride to his friend's house because no one was able to come and pick him up. He was sitting on the curb across the street. You might have already guessed what I did. I threw on some clothes and took him. He had the trash bag of clothes the officers allowed him to get and put them in the trunk. On the way there, he berated me for calling the cops and for leaving him outside for over three hours. I let him talk because I didn't have much to say. It was a very long drive for a short distance. When I pulled up, my parting words were for him was to learn how to keep his hands to himself. I took him back a week later.

When he came back, I started thinking that maybe we needed to be in our own place. When it came time for my mom and I to renew our lease, we opted out. Instead, we choose separate apartments in the same complex. I foolishly thought this was what we needed. The name-calling wasn't as frequent, and he was keeping his hands to himself. Sex was only when he wanted, and my prayers intensified but with a slight variation.

Heavenly Father, I know Derrick is not the man you created for me. I pray that you can change him for the next woman. Give me the strength I need to walk away. Amen.

That became my prayer all the time. One night, I had a dream that I was having a bowel movement. I jumped up out of the bed scared I just took a dump on myself and ran to the bathroom. My panties were empty. I grabbed my phone and looked up the meaning of the dream. One version I read said to dream of defecation symbolizes the removal of waste from your life. I went back to the bedroom and looked at Derrick lying there asleep and concluded that he was the waste I needed to remove. I prayed and went back to sleep.

With requests for sex being denied, my tolerance for Derrick became nonexistent but I still wanted to try. My mom had already left for my sisters for the summer, and I was joining for the 4th of July holiday. On the 3rd, there was a fireworks display that we planned on taking the girls to. We were going to go out for lunch around one, take in a movie, then come back home to eat before leaving for the park at seven. He took the car that day because I was off, but he had to work until noon.

By three pm, the girls and I walked over to the supermarket to get something to eat since he was not back and did not state a time he would be coming back. By eight pm, I found myself thanking God that I did not tell the girls the plans. By ten I had put them to bed and started packing for my sisters. At 11:30 p.m., he finally walked through the door high and drunk.

Silence Can Be a Trigger

"Why are you not speaking to me? You mad."
"Let's see, we had a whole day planned and you are just coming home."
"So." he says with a smile on his face.
"So? You stopped taking my calls and you had my car."
"I'm coming with you."
"No, you are not."
"Why not?"
"Because you are not. I don't want you on this trip. You have no concern for anyone but yourself."
"I'm coming with you and you can't tell me I'm not." I head to the balcony to smoke and he followed me.
"What time are we leaving?"
Silence
"Are you mad at me?"
Silence
"Don't be mad. I just let time get away from me hanging out. I got some good weed and wanted to share. You want some?" I head inside to brush my teeth and get ready for bed.
"Bitch you hear me talking to you."
Silence

After checking on the girls to make sure they were sleeping, I continue ignoring his taunts and snuggled into bed. He lifts the mattress to toss me out. When I get up off the floor, he is standing in front of me. I get back in bed, and he snatches the pillows from underneath me and asks me again if I'm mad. I start to wonder why it seems that when I am trying to avoid a fight, my silence makes matters worse?

"Derrick, I have a long drive ahead of me and I need to get some sleep. Please leave me alone."
"No. Why? I'm doing the driving."

"You are not going. You are not welcomed on this trip."
"You mean I'm not welcomed at your sister's house. Is that it?"
"Look at it however you want. You are not going now please leave me alone."

Next thing I know, he picked up his bat that he keeps by the bed and hit the headboard right over my head. I jump out the bed and check on the girls to make sure the noise didn't wake them. He followed me, so I hurry and leave their room. I go back into the bedroom to try and get some sleep. I won't even turn the light off on him.

He lifts the mattress up again all the while calling me names. He takes the pillows before I can get back into bed. As I stand next to my side of the bed he comes over and pushes me down. As I start to get back up, he jumps on me and pins my arms down as he climbs up to my chest to sit. Kicking has become more work, so I stop. I start trying to move him off me by twisting my body but with him on my chest holding on to my arms, it is becoming futile. He gets both of my arms over my head to where he can hold them with one arm. I have been in this position before and mentally flashback to that snowy night. Now I am livid and ready to fight.

With his free hand, he slaps my face taking turns on each side. He begins to unbuckle his belt to give me, "A golden shower right on your face."

Lord, if you get me out of this, I will walk away and not look back. I pray to myself.

He changes his mind about the golden shower and determines I need a beating instead. However, with him trying to use the belt on me, he loses his grip on my arm, and I reach for his hair and directs his body to move off me. When I get up, some of his hair is in my hand. He lunges for me, and I push his face away scratching him in the process. Neither one of us is speaking. We stand there breathing heavily, waiting to see what the other is going to do. He touches his face, and his hand comes away with blood.

I make the mistake of looking at the bleeding scratch on his arm and almost missed when he pulled back his fist to strike. I moved at the last second and his fist connected with my left ear. The power in that punch makes me unsteady and confused. I try to leave the room, but he reaches the door first. With my balance a little off, he throws me to the bed and starts to choke me. I start scratching his face and grab the side of his neck and dig in causing him to let me go. As I stand up, he pushes me, and I push back with my foot. He grabs my hair and pulls me to the floor. I am grabbing at his arms trying to get up. He lets me go.

Once I can stand, we are doing this staring/breathing match by the door. There is a knock, and I yell for whoever it is to go back to bed.

"Mommy, what are you doing?"
"Derrick and I was moving the bed now go back to sleep."

He exits the room and heads for the balcony. I go and tuck the girls back in and grab my phone and car keys to hide them in the linen closet. I decide to take a shower. In the shower, I realize my vulnerability if he decides to come in and continue the fight. I wash up fast. As I am rinsing off, he comes in. I quickly step out because I do not want a fight in a wet tub. He asks for the car keys. I tell him I don't know where they are. He was the last one to have them. He goes back out to the balcony stopping first in the kitchen to get a beer.

While he is out there, I throw on the clothes I had out to travel in and get the girls up and dressed. As they get dressed, I pray for their safety while I load the car. I carry as much as I can without falling down the steps because I didn't want to have to make several trips with the girls upstairs. I throw everything into the trunk without taking the time for neatness. I run upstairs just as Derrick is coming back in. I tell the girls, "Go use the bathroom because we are leaving for Auntie's house right now." I thank God for packing earlier and having everything already ready. By the time the girls finished in the bathroom, he is sitting on the sofa drinking a beer, looking like his face just went through a windshield.

Autumn: "Derrick why is your face bleeding?"
"Girls. Take a good look at Derrick. This will be the last time you ever see him."
Teagan: "Why?"
"You see his face?"
"Yes." They say in unison.
"Look at him and know, no man is to ever put their hands on you not even one time because one time is too many and if they do, they better not get the best of you. Now let's go."

Before I lock the door, I turn to a silent Derrick. "You and your belongings need to be out of my place before I return on the 6th. I do not want to have you removed myself."

And with that, I locked the door on the marriage between Derrick and myself. It was 4:38 in the morning.

Damn Luther Vandross

I would be lying if I told you it was an easy transition. It wasn't.

When I returned home some days later, Derrick was gone. Most of his clothes were gone, but he still had a set of keys since he locked up the place. This meant that I still had to have a conversation with him.

Once I texted him to let him know I was back, he informed me that he was coming to pick up the bed. I asked if I could buy it from him to which he replied. "A bitch like you deserves to sleep on the floor." Two days later, he and a friend came over during my lunch break to remove the rest of his items including the mattress and bedframe. My room was empty. The only furniture left was my leather chair, nightstand and lamp.

The next month, my mom and I moved into our separate apartments across the street from each other. At first, this move felt like a waste since there wasn't a marriage needing a start over. I thought Derrick and I needed our own space to build our marriage. A change of scenery. To grow as husband, wife and stepfather. A place to develop our own rhythm of life with our new family. Deep down I knew that no location change would divert his abusive ways. It was who he was. After all, during all these fights, he was still attending the court-ordered anger management classes that clearly weren't working.

About a month after getting settled in, I made the mistake of taking a long bath with Luther Vandross's *If Only for One Night* and *If This World Were Mine* on repeat.

I called Derrick and invited him over. He borrowed a car and came over with a twelve pack in hand. I wanted to be with someone, and he wanted to talk. We went on the balcony. The more we talked, the more he drank. By the end of the night, my anticipation of getting laid was extinguished. All he wanted to do was sleep on the pallet of blankets that was temporarily my bed and rest.

Not even hold me. Just rest.

Honestly, I didn't want him to hold me. I wanted him to fuck me. As he slept, I went back out to the balcony to smoke and ask God what the hell was wrong with me? Why did I even invite him over? Did I really want sex? Or did I want to throw it in his face to show him where he could have been living? To rub it in that he could no longer have me? It couldn't have been the last one because I was the one to call him over. I wanted him. Or at least his equipment that was better than the overpriced rabbit that did not satisfy. Then, I came to my senses and went back in to wake him up and kick him out.

"You know you are one sick bitch."
"Excuse me?'
"You are sick, and you need to seek help. You only called me because you wanted to fuck."
"You are talking about me needing help? I'm not the one with the problem of keeping their hands to themselves."
"I might have anger issues, but you are using sex to deal with those rapes. You need to deal with being raped so you won't need sex all the time."
"Are you fucking kidding me? You saying I want sex too much?"
"Night bitch."
"Thank you for not fucking me so I'll have no regrets."
"I regret you."

That was the last thing he said to my face before crossing the threshold of my apartment.

I laughed all the way to the kitchen to grab a remaining beer. Laughed as I lit up out on the balcony and asked God if he heard all of that. Out loud I asked him. To me, it was the funniest conversation I had to date. I laughed myself to sleep that night. And the next day I laughed as I told it to Asha and my sister. The problem was that both did not return the laughter.

They basically asked the same thing. Is there truth to what he said? My answer to both was, "No. I dealt with them." They weren't any help. They didn't share my view of the ridiculousness of his claims. This pissed me off. How dare they insinuate that there could possibly be some truth to what he said. I was always like this for as long as I can remember. Before any rapes. And yes dear reader. If you are thinking that I only told you about one, I did. It wasn't a typographical error.

Night on the Town

I'm going to make this short because let's face it, you have been through a lot with me thus far. But here it goes.

Two of my co-workers, Mike and Yvette wanted to go to the club. I was twenty-two and Kamar was going to stay with my mom. We made plans to meet at McDonalds in Downtown Brooklyn.

By the time I showed up, Mike was there with his twin brother and another friend. We were waiting on Yvette when I received a page from her. She changed her mind and decided to stay home due to a headache. At the payphone, I informed Mike of the change in plans and that I was going to go home. I allowed him to reverse my thinking even though I was no longer comfortable.

Fast-forward to the club where I purchased the first beer and let Mike buy me the next one. Then I felt nauseous and dizzy and went to the bathroom to force myself to vomit.

Here is where things start coming in bits and pieces. I know his brother brought me a Corona and water. I drank most of the beer and some water to help wash the taste of vomit. Not sure how much longer we stayed but I do know I needed help leaving the club and I still had my water.

In the parking lot, I can recall being hot and laughing as his brother stroked my thigh while telling me to drink the water. But I couldn't open it. My balance was off. I remember Mike getting in the car and his brother touching me between my legs saying I was wet and me slapping his hand away.

And it was pitch dark outside.

I must have passed out because the next thing I recall from Mike is his telling me the brownstone we just passed was where the Notorious B.I.G lived. Out again because Mike was waking me up telling me that I'm home. I was confused because my watch read that it was after 7 a.m. Mike handed me my panties, and I asked why I didn't have them on? I exited his car with panties and purse in hand and closed his door. He was gone before I stepped onto the sidewalk.

Taking a very real walk of shame to my door while trying to figure out what I was ashamed of? What did I do? My head was aching and I felt sick. I sat down on the ledge of the first-floor window wondering why my vagina and ass were tender.

At that point, the only events I remembered was screaming from someone sticking or trying to stick their dick in my ass. *And in another goddamn basement!*

It dawned on me they had to have put something in my drink because there was no way I would have gotten drunk off just three beers. I couldn't cry because I was too busy trying to get my mind to work. I thought about going to the hospital to have my blood tested but quickly decided against it. I had already been down that road of blame, guilt and shame and wasn't going to put myself through that again. I was already berating myself for putting me in the situation in the first place.

Once she canceled, I should have gone home. I should have listened to my intuition. *If this was a Lifetime movie, I would have been yelling for her to go home and damn anybody's hurt feelings.*

Monday came, and I went to work wanting answers. He never seemed to be available. It wasn't until the next day that I asked him point blank did he or his brother put something in my drink. He said, "No."

What was I thinking? An all-out confession? I told him with the straightest face void of any anger or any emotion.

"You or your brother spiked my drink and raped me. I know it and you know it. There is no other explanation for me not remembering more than I do. And I probably would have been down for a threesome if I could have been in control of me and the environment. You, your brother and possibly your friend took that option away from me."

I turned away went back to my desk and proceeded to work. Before the week was over, he quit giving me the confirmation I needed. Yvette and I were no longer as close as we once were. She confirmed she was leaving the house, then not show up because you suddenly get a headache. There's Tylenol for that. Yes. I partially blamed her. Even if it was wrong for me to do so.

About a two years later, I saw him at the train station, and he approached me.

"I want to say sorry for my brother. We went out with another girl, and he spiked her drink. He admitted to spiking your also."

"So, what you are saying is that you knew your brother spiked my drink and you proceeded to take advantage and now you are admitting to me that you both raped another woman. Because Mike, that is exactly what you did." I said getting all up in his personal space.

"Yes. I'm sorry. I should have known you weren't consenting because she was just as out of it as you were. May I ask you a question." I just stare at him. "A few months later, my brother was a victim of violence....." I preceded to walk away as he is still speaking.

Now. Back to where I left off.

They didn't know what they were talking about. I had to take this to the only person who knew me better than I knew myself. God.

A New Theory

During the waiting period for divorce, I decided to take a long look at myself. I knew the reason for my appetite for sex was not what Derrick said, but a need to rid myself of emotions.

Seeking temporary relief from life and all the feelings it brings with it.

This needed to change, and it was beyond me to do so. I was able to acknowledge that God is the only one who could fix this. The problem was where to start. Going to church all these years didn't bring about a change. Praying and singing didn't do it. Worshipping and praising yielded no results. But to be fair and honest, I can't recall if I ever asked God to take this part of me away.

I enjoyed it too much to even think of letting it go.

Trying to find a beginning point was frustrating. I was stressing myself out, which was making me want sex, which made me call Derrick. We ended up in an argument before I could even ask him to come over. This cycle continued for almost a week. I had to recruit my girlfriend for help. Asha agreed that every time I felt the need to call him, I was to call her instead.

A working friend with a job and life of her own isn't always able to pick up the phone. Back to square one. I needed a friend whom I could call no matter what time of day or night it was, and I had no one like that. At least that was my initial thought, until I remembered Jesus and how He was my friend.

I called Him. Nothing happened. I was sexually frustrated and annoyed with the feeling.

Getting ticked off at Jesus because He wasn't answering my calls. Here I was, listening to sermons posted on YouTube, reading the scriptures, meditating on them for life application and being ignored by the Son of God.

Listening to the radio one evening, there was a discussion about soul ties. I have never heard this phrase before. I was intrigued enough to not change the channel. The person was saying how when we have intercourse with someone, a piece of their soul remains with us. Soul tie is the spiritual connection between two people who have been physically intimate with one another.

From that night through several weeks, it seemed this soul tie theory was everywhere. I was watching sermons about it. People were on the gospel station talking about. Why did I never hear this before? It was an interesting viewpoint. I started thinking about all the men I had been with. The thought of all these connections having a piece of me and I of them made my head spin. It disgusted me when I thought about the types of men, I gave myself to and what of them was lurking in my spirit. I needed to understand more.

I read articles from various religious groups and people. They all said the same thing. A connection or emotional/spiritual bond between you and the person you are physically intimate with, that lasts long after the relationship is over. The phrase soul tie is not in the Bible. Nor is the concept of it.

One ideology pulled from scripture, like, *1 Corinthians 6:16 Or do you not know that he who is joined to a harlot is one body with her? For, "the two," He says, "shall become one flesh."* This scripture speaks of bodies uniting as one, not souls. Soul tie may not be directly from the Bible, but its idea opened my eyes.

It caused me to redirect my request to God and change the conversations I had with Him. I asked God to cleanse me of all bonding connections. To me, this cleanse required delving more into the word and reflection with Jesus. I wondered if this way of looking at sex when I was younger would have prevented me from ever losing my virginity.

The thought of someone else's soul occupying even a sliver of space in mine when they are long gone, and I can't even remember their names is disgusting.

Scary thinking of it as an adult, that it most likely would have petrified me as a child. If it didn't and I still went down this same path, maybe the choice of partners would have been better. If I understood that I wasn't just giving over my body but my soul, maybe my criteria would have been higher. Maybe I would just wait for my husband.

For weeks this was my focus. Slowly, I stopped concentrating on an inner cleansing and just went on with reading my Bible and listening to sermons. Studying the scriptures and letting them change me for the better through understanding. Staring into the mirror learning to love myself. Telling me that I was beautiful.

Falling in love with the reflection and the person that gazed back at me. Telling her that she was worth living for. God thought she was because He created her, and I was her. Reversing the childhood feelings of ugliness. I was in my thirties building my self-esteem.

Mid-way through 2014, I had my first realization that I wasn't missing sex. It shocked me, and I dismissed it. Didn't want to jinx it. Then I got behind on my bills, and the stress didn't drive me into anyone's bed. It didn't even come up for consideration. I caught up on the bills without even wanting a man to celebrate with.

Tested. This guy started hitting on me and talking about all things sexual. I feel into the trap and talked and texted dirty. This went on for four days before I snapped out of it. I texted him that

I believed he was a test to interrupt my path, and I failed. He wanted to know what I meant but I didn't elaborate. He believed in God, and I knew he would get what I was saying.

I prayed for God to remove the temptation from me and to provide me with strength to resist. The next day I received a sex text. I replied that I am not playing anymore and that he was fine enough to find someone else to mess with. It ended just like that. God gave me strength to walk away

Now I will not tell you it has always been easy. Since separating from Derrick, I have had two sexual encounters. One in 2015 and one in 2017. Both times it was just because. Not because something was going on and I needed to channel the energy. Not to relieve stress. Truly just because. I wanted to make sure I still worked and was able to get turned on.

Chase came to spend time with the girls in 2015, and we did it for old times' sake. It was uneventful and meant nothing.

Dear reader. My friend. Can you guess who was passing through in 2017? I'll wait.

If you guessed Nathan, you would be right. *I saw you shake your head.* Again. No emotional reason why. Just because.

Let me end by telling you why I feel the marriage to Derrick was one of the best mistakes I could have made, minus the abuse.

Isaiah 61:3 To console those who mourn in Zion, to give them beauty for ashes, The oil of joy for mourning, The garment of praise for the spirit of heaviness; That they may be called trees of righteousness, The planting of the Lord, that He may be glorified."

This scripture tells of how God will turn our mess into His glory. He will give us beauty for the ashes of life. He took my farce of marriage and turned it for my good. He took a bad decision and used it to cleanse me of, dare I say, sexual addiction?

If I never married Derrick, I do believe I would be adding bodies and giving away more of me.

Maybe the theory of soul tie would not have made me open my eyes to my behavior. God kept me alive in that and used it to change me. He answered my prayers. I can rejoice in who I used to be because I USED to be! How do I know I am changed?

In 2015, after finalizing my divorce. I wanted to celebrate by going to church. I didn't want to celebrate with a fun night in someone's bed. I was changed and didn't get the memo. It just happened. God made the change without calling me to the meeting. It wasn't instant like being at the altar. It was just over time. I still find men sexy and look at them in a sexual way, but it just doesn't hold my focus for long.

What does are fantasies about their mentality and aspirations. If they pray and have a relationship with the Trinity. Are they worshippers? Are they emotionally mature? Can they make me laugh, encourage me and speak life into my dreams. I envision us with our bodies entwined reading the Bible together or discussing scriptures. Whatever image it is, I always follow it up with this prayer:

Lord. You know I love you and want to grow deeper with you each day. But I don't want to be with You and You alone. Prepare me for the one after your own heart whom you have for me. May he strengthen my walk with you, through his walk with you. And may he enjoy the exploration and frequency of sex. Don't be shy about speeding it up either. I think?

Thank you in advance and Amen.

The Last Dance

In 2023, as I was writing the chapter We Have An Issue, *yet again*, my phone rang. The caller ID said Nathan. Laughing, I answered it.

"Hey Chelle."
"It's been a long time. Good to hear your voice. How are you."
"I'm coming to NC this weekend and would like to see you."
"I was literally just writing your chapter."

We met up for dinner, caught up on our lives and if we'd like to take another shot at an us. With Kamar building a life in another state, Autumn working full-time and Teagan off to college, I was willing to see if we could do it. I told him this would be our final chance. If we didn't work out, there would be no more rounds to go.

The first few months were bliss. I was going to his place every other weekend. It was the first time I wanted to get pregnant. Wanted to give him the child I terminated. *After reading all you have read, you should know how much of a big deal this was for me.*

I actually wanted to get pregnant. I don't know if it was the need to give him something he wanted that was born out of our love. Or just to have his baby. A way, a reason for us to work hard at staying together. Either way, I was ready.

On father's day, we unintentionally tired. While waiting to see if conception took place, I realized I wanted the idea more than the reality of what that would mean. My children and his were grown. I wanted to relish my freedom more than being tied down with a baby. And thankfully, God said "Nope."

I was also willing and ready to take on his last name. That is how in love I was. Nathan and I were committed to each other, and I finally was with the man that has always had a place in my heart.

No more what ifs. I was all in. Ready to build a life with him.

Then about the fourth month, cracks started to show. He was not the man that had the qualities I was praying for. The man that happily attended church when he lived with us no longer believed. He approached everything as if he was a running the streets. Any problem that I spoke to him about, the other person was always called a bitch or nigga.

I felt like conversations didn't flow naturally between us. It was always fuck this or fuck that. Slowly, his needs took precedence over mine. We didn't go out and started arguing all the time. And as life dealt us blows personally, the way we approached it were polar opposites.

His way included violence and unnecessary profanity. Mine was encouragement and mild profanity. But I didn't want to walk away. I wanted to work through our differences. However big they were.

We were both disappointing each other with the expectations of how we needed the other person to be there. So, after almost two years, we parted ways.

And I regret nothing.

I needed this chance with him. I now know that we can't be together. We were drastically different, and our aspirations were not equally yoked. The what if has been answered. The chapter closed. No more wondering. No more not totally giving of myself to someone else because Nathan was always in the corner of my mind and heart. He had been evicted.

I look forward to finding out what love looks like when the next man gets to have all of me. I am thankful I answered his call and only hope he finds the woman that will be able to give him everything he desires, because I want the same for myself.

And Lord, I am ready now. Please and Thank You. Amen.

With Sincere Thanks,

My children. We went through stormy seas, high winds, and beautiful sunsets. Yet, you have grown up to be the ones who inspire me the most. The ones who I look up to. You have fulfilled my prayers that each of you will be better than me and continue to do so. I only hope you can be a little proud of me.

My angels. Your short stay does not negate the love I have for you even now. When my time comes, I pray you will be there to greet me in the arms of TT.

My daughter-in-law. Thank you for choosing to love my son. I count myself Blessed to have you as a part of my crew.

Out of the twelve, Jesus had three main road dogs. My three all begin with the letter K. These women have listened to my tears, my heartaches, and my triumphs. They are the definition of friendship. They have kept me honest, let me know when I was in the wrong, and encouraged me when I couldn't find the strength to encourage myself. They each make life more bearable. I love you and will forever protect our friendship. *You know who you are even if I don't spell out your name.*

To my Auntie who recommend her friend to edit my life. Thank you so much. To my editor, your critiques were invaluable, and your positive comments meant everything to me. I thank you.

To my cousin and his family. Thank you for opening your home to us. Thank you for your patience and understanding. Thank you for loving me enough to want us to have a safe space to heal and start over.

To my co-worker. Your enthusiasm to read my book for me and pushing me to finish in time for your vacation was a fire I desperately needed. Thank you.

To the man I met at the park who is always right. Thank you for introducing me to dating. You are the man of my prayers. The one I thought my choices have kept me from. The type of man I thought I was never good enough to have. That he would remain a prayer. Thank you for showing me I am worth it.

To every person who decided to take a chance and read about my life, Thank You. To anyone who wants to judge and smear my name because of my decisions, remember they were mine and mine alone. This book was an assignment from God. He did not bring me through everything for my testimonies to stay with me. So, take it up with Him. *Amen?* Amen.

And finally, my mother. Thank you for the gift of the laptop. Sorry my journey outlasted its lifespan.

Psalms 102: 17 & 18: He shall regard the prayer of the destitute, and shall not despise their prayer. This will be written for the generation to come, that a people yet to be created may praise the Lord.

I truly hope you will answer the door if you haven't already.

www.ingramcontent.com/pod-product-compliance
Lightning Source LLC
Chambersburg PA
CBHW070643160426
43194CB00009B/1559